Swift Pocket Reference

D1025689

Anthony Gray

Beijing · Cambridge · Farnham · Köln · Sebastopol · Tokyo

Swift Pocket Reference

by Anthony Gray

Copyright © 2015 Anthony Gray. All rights reserved.

Printed in the United States of America.

Published by O'Reilly Media, Inc., 1005 Gravenstein Highway North, Sebastopol, CA 95472.

O'Reilly books may be purchased for educational, business, or sales promotional use. Online editions are also available for most titles (*http://safaribook sonline.com*). For more information, contact our corporate/institutional sales department: 800-998-9938 or corporate@oreilly.com .

Editor: Rachel Roumeliotis
Production Editor: Matthew Hacker
Copyeditor: Bob Russell, Octal Publishing, Inc.
Proofreader: Jasmine Kwityn
Indexer: WordCo Indexing Services, Inc.
Interior Designer: David Futato
Cover Designer: Ellie Volckhausen
Illustrator: Rebecca Demarest

December 2014:   First Edition

Revision History for the First Edition
          2014-11-26:   First Release

See   *http://oreilly.com/catalog/errata.csp?isbn=9781491915424*   for   release details.

978-1-491-91542-4

[LSI]

Table of Contents

Introduction	1
Conventions Used in This Book	2
Using Code Examples	2
Safari® Books Online	3
How to Contact Us	4
Acknowledgments	4
Getting Started with Swift	5
A Taste of Swift	11
Basic Language Features	14
Types	17
Variables and Constants	21
Tuples	26
Operators	29
Strings and Characters	38
Arrays	42
Dictionaries	47
Functions	51
Closures	57
Optionals	63
Program Flow	69

Classes	80
Structures	108
Enumerations	112
Access Control	119
Extensions	123
Checking and Casting Types	127
Protocols	131
Memory Management	142
Generics	149
Operator Overloading	155
Ranges, Intervals, and Strides	160
Global Functions	163
Index	169

Swift Pocket Reference

Introduction

Swift is an exciting new language from Apple, first announced at the Apple Worldwide Developers Conference (WWDC) in June 2014. The language started life as the brainchild of Chris Lattner, director of Apple's Developer Tools Department, and is the next step in the evolution of Apple's software development ecosystem.

Swift brings with it many modern language features, including type safety, generics, type inference, closures, tuples, automatic memory management, and support for Unicode (for character and string values as well as for identifiers). You can use a mixture of Swift and Objective-C in a single project, and either language can call APIs implemented in the other.

The challenge for anyone learning (or even writing about) Swift is that the language is still evolving. Apple has stated that the language specification is not final, and the syntax and feature set will change.

Despite the uncertainty of a changing language, Swift shows great promise. It follows on from the company's other major developer tools initiatives (all led by Lattner) including LLVM, Clang, LLDB, ARC, and a series of extensions to Objective-C, and it's clear that Apple sees it as the future language of choice for iOS and OS X software development.

Conventions Used in This Book

The following typographical conventions are used in this book:

Italic

> Indicates new terms, URLs, email addresses, filenames, and file extensions.

`Constant width`

> Used for program listings, as well as within paragraphs to refer to program elements such as variable or function names, databases, data types, environment variables, statements, and keywords.

`Constant width bold`

> Shows commands or other text that should be typed literally by the user.

`Constant width italic`

> Shows text that should be replaced with user-supplied values or by values determined by context.

NOTE

This element signifies a general note.

Using Code Examples

This book is here to help you get your job done. In general, if example code is offered with this book, you may use it in your programs and documentation. You do not need to contact us for permission unless you're reproducing a significant portion of the code. For example, writing a program that uses several chunks of code from this book does not require permission. Selling or distributing a CD-ROM of examples from O'Reilly

---

books does require permission. Answering a question by citing this book and quoting example code does not require permission. Incorporating a significant amount of example code from this book into your product's documentation does require permission.

We appreciate, but do not require, attribution. An attribution usually includes the title, author, publisher, and ISBN. For example: "*Swift Pocket Reference* by Anthony Gray (O'Reilly). Copyright 2015 Anthony Gray, 978-1-491-91542-4."

If you feel your use of code examples falls outside fair use or the permission given above, feel free to contact us at *permissions@oreilly.com*.

Safari® Books Online

Safari Books Online is an on-demand digital library that delivers expert content in both book and video form from the world's leading authors in technology and business.

Technology professionals, software developers, web designers, and business and creative professionals use Safari Books Online as their primary resource for research, problem solving, learning, and certification training.

Safari Books Online offers a range of plans and pricing for enterprise, government, education, and individuals.

Members have access to thousands of books, training videos, and prepublication manuscripts in one fully searchable database from publishers like O'Reilly Media, Prentice Hall Professional, Addison-Wesley Professional, Microsoft Press, Sams, Que, Peachpit Press, Focal Press, Cisco Press, John Wiley & Sons, Syngress, Morgan Kaufmann, IBM Redbooks, Packt, Adobe Press, FT Press, Apress, Manning, New Riders, McGraw-Hill, Jones & Bartlett, Course Technology, and hundreds more. For more information about Safari Books Online, please visit us online.

How to Contact Us

Please address comments and questions concerning this book to the publisher:

> O'Reilly Media, Inc.
> 1005 Gravenstein Highway North
> Sebastopol, CA 95472
> 800-998-9938 (in the United States or Canada)
> 707-829-0515 (international or local)
> 707-829-0104 (fax)

We have a web page for this book, where we list errata, examples, and any additional information. You can access this page at *http://bit.ly/swift_pocket_ref*.

To comment or ask technical questions about this book, send email to *bookquestions@oreilly.com*.

For more information about our books, courses, conferences, and news, see our website at *http://www.oreilly.com*.

Find us on Facebook: *http://facebook.com/oreilly*

Follow us on Twitter: *http://twitter.com/oreillymedia*

Watch us on YouTube: *http://www.youtube.com/oreillymedia*

Acknowledgments

I would like to thank Paris Buttfield-Addison for urging me (repeatedly) to write this book. He and his partner-in-crime, Jon Manning, suffer from boundless optimism and seem to regard "no" as a challenge rather than as a defeat. I'd also like to thank Rachel Roumeliotis and the other fine folk at O'Reilly for having faith in me and for shepherding the project through to completion. Special thanks also go to the readers of the early release editions, who took the time to provide feedback and suggestions for improvement, for which I'm deeply grateful.

Getting Started with Swift

To code in the Swift language, you need to be using Xcode 6.1 or later (available free on the Mac App Store), which runs in either OS X 10.9 (Mavericks) or OS X 10.10 (Yosemite). You might also consider signing up as a registered Apple developer (with free and paid tiers) to gain access to a wealth of documentation and other developer resources at *https://developer.apple.com*.

You can use the version of Swift built into Xcode 6.1 to compile programs that will run on OS X 10.9 and OS X 10.10, and on iOS 7 and iOS 8.

After you have downloaded and installed Xcode 6.1, go ahead and run it and allow it to install the various tools that are bundled with it. When installation is complete, there are a number of ways that you can get started with Swift:

- Click File → New Project to create a new Xcode project. The project wizard opens and offers you the choice of using Swift or Objective-C as the language for the project.

- Click File → New Playground to create a new playground document. Playgrounds are single-window dynamic environments in which you can experiment with Swift language features and see results instantly alongside the code you enter.

- Create a Swift script and run it from the command line in the OS X terminal.

- Use the Swift Read-Evaluate-Print-Loop (REPL) in the OS X terminal.

Let's look at the REPL, Swift scripting, and playgrounds in more detail.

NOTE

As of this writing, some features of Swift and Xcode 6.1 are still unstable. It is likely that you will encounter instability associated with Swift playgrounds as well as with Xcode's autocomplete feature and syntax highlighting. In playgrounds, the result of an expression might not always be displayed alongside it in the results sidebar; instead, it might appear alongside an earlier line. Occasionally, you might need to quit and restart Xcode to get it back to a sensible state.

The Swift REPL

The Swift REPL provides command-line access to Swift and behaves like an interpreter. You can declare variables and constants, define functions, evaluate expressions, and use most other language features; they will be compiled and executed immediately.

Multiple Xcode installations

If you have more than one installation of Xcode on your computer, you will need to use the **xcode-select** command to choose the Xcode 6 environment as the active developer directory. In the terminal, type the following command:

```
sudo xcode-select -s /Applications/Xcode.app
```

When prompted, provide your administrator username and password. If you have installed Xcode in a different location or changed its name, replace the path in the command with the location and name of your installed release.

Starting the REPL

To start the REPL so that you can test Swift language features, use the following command:

```
xcrun swift
```

If you've never used Xcode before, you might see an authentication prompt from a process called *Developer Tools Access* (see Figure 1), prompting you for a username and password. You will need to enter an administrator username and password to continue. After you enter these, you might see the following error message (on OS X 10.9):

```
error: failed to launch REPL process: process
exited with status -1 (lost connection)
```

At this point, type the **xcrun swift** command again. This time, the REPL should start normally.

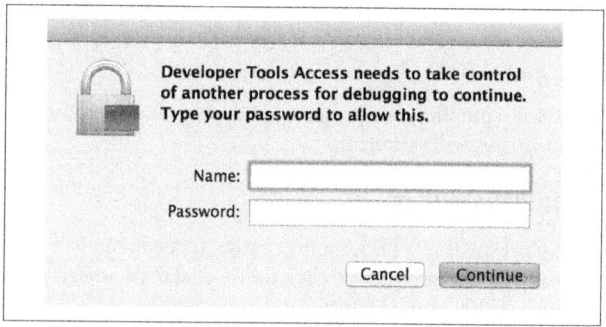

Figure 1. The Developer Tools Access prompt

When the REPL starts, you will see the following output:

```
Welcome to Swift!  Type :help for assistance.
  1>
```

You're now ready to try your first code in Swift. Try the printl n function:

```
  1> println ("Hello, World")
Hello, World
  2>
```

The REPL is a great way to test Swift features and experiment with the language.

Swift as a Scripting Language

You can use Swift as a scripting language, much like Perl, Python, or Ruby. To use Swift in this manner, ensure the first line of the script contains the path to the Swift "interpreter." If you want to try Swift in this way, type the following into a text file named *hello.swift*:

```
#!/usr/bin/swift

println ("Hello, World")
```

Next, ensure that the script is marked as executable with a chmod command:

```
chmod u+x hello.swift
```

Now, run the script as follows:

```
./hello.swift
```

Swift will compile your program, and assuming there are no syntax errors, will execute it.

Swift Playgrounds

To explore Swift in a playground, on the Xcode menu bar, click File → New Playground, or click the "Get started with a playground" option in the Welcome to Xcode window.

You are then prompted to enter a playground name (which becomes the saved document's name) and a platform (iOS or OS X), as demonstrated in Figure 2.

Once you've entered your playground name and selected your platform, click Next. You will then be prompted to select a location to which to save the file. When the file has been saved, you see the initial playground window, shown in Figure 3.

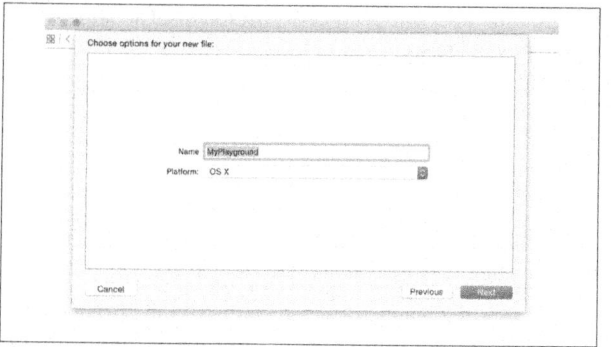

Figure 2. Creating a Swift playground

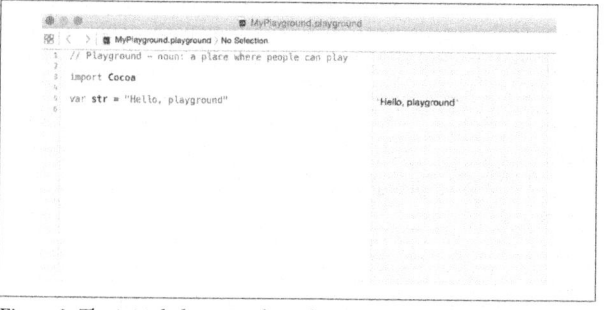

Figure 3. The initial playground window

The playground template imports either the Cocoa or UIKit Framework, depending on whether you selected OS X or iOS as your playground platform. This means that you can experiment not just with basic Swift language features, but also with many of the features provided by the framework, such as drawing views and images, and even implementing basic animations.

The playground also displays a line of code:

```
var str = "Hello, playground"
```

To the right of that code is the value "Hello, playground". This demonstrates one of the most useful features of the playground: the result of every expression displays alongside it in the results sidebar.

Below the existing text, type the following:

```
for var i=0; i<10; i++
{
    println (i)
}
```

The results sidebar now displays the text "(10 times)" to confirm the number of executions of the loop.

If you hover the pointer over the entries in the results sidebar (Figure 4), you'll see two symbols. The eye-like symbol provides a *Quick Look* view of the value (this includes viewers for complex data such as strings, arrays, dictionaries, images, views, URLs, and more). The button symbol opens another sidebar in the window called the *Timeline*.

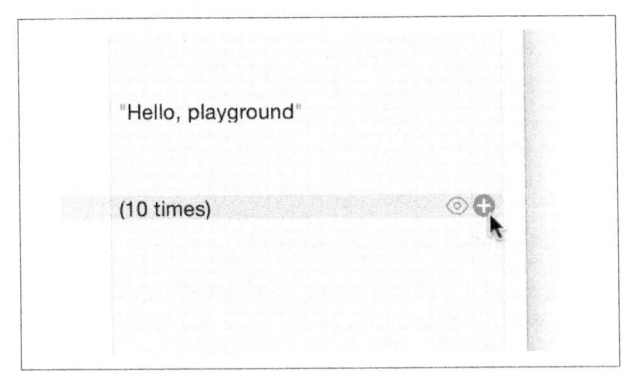

Figure 4. Accessing Quick Look and the Timeline from the results sidebar

The Timeline can show how values have changed over time as well as console output (e.g., text output by the `println` function).

You can also open the Timeline by going to the Xcode menu bar and clicking View → Assistant Editor → Show Assistant

Editor, or you can use the keyboard shortcut Command-Option-Return.

NOTE

For an excellent introduction to playgrounds, see the recording of session 408 (Swift Playgrounds) from the 2014 Worldwide Developers Conference (*http://bit.ly/2014_wwdc*).

A Taste of Swift

Let's dive right in. What follows is a simple program written in Swift. Work through carefully to get a sense of some of the features of the language.

The first thing our program does is define a pair of arrays: one named users, and another named ages for those users. This is meant to represent raw input of disassociated data that needs to be merged and then used as the basis of a report:

```
// some raw data to process
var users = ["xavier", "ryan", "brenda", "james", "sarah"]
var ages = [32, 28, 24, 41, 19]
```

The next section of code is a pair of extensions to the String type. Swift has built-in support for Unicode strings, but it also has a very flexible extension mechanism with which you can add new features to the language—even to built-in types. Our extension adds two new member functions to the String type that can take a string and return a copy that is padded with leading or trailing spaces to a specified width:

```
// add some extensions to the String type
extension String
{
    func leadingSpaces(width: Int) -> String
    {
        var s = "\(self)"
        for i in countElements(s)..<width
```

```
        {
            s = " " + s
        }
        return s
    }

    func trailingSpaces (width: Int) -> String
    {
        var s = "\(self)"
        for i in countElements(s)..<width
        {
            s = s + " "
        }
        return s
    }
}
```

Next, we declare a dictionary merged. This is an associative array of key/value pairs to store each user's name and age. We also declare a variable, totalAge, to sum all of the ages so that we can later calculate the average age of all users:

```
// a dictionary to store merged input
var merged = [String: Int]()
var totalAge = 0.0;
```

With the dictionary defined, we now iterate over the two input arrays, merging them into the merged dictionary. The dictionary utilizes the user's name as the key, and the user's age as the value:

```
// merge the two arrays into a dictionary
for var i=0; i < ages.count; i++
{
    merged[users[i]] = ages[i]
}
```

Now that we have a dictionary containing all of the raw input, it's time to generate a report. We want to list the users in sorted order, and we want to print each user's age alongside their name, using trailing and leading spaces so that the names are left-aligned under one another and the ages are right-aligned:

```
// interate over the dictionary in sorted order
// and generate a report
for user in sorted(merged.keys)
```

```
{
    let age = merged[user]!
    totalAge += Double(age)
    let paddedUser = user.trailingSpaces(10)
    let paddedAge = "\(age)".leadingSpaces(3)
    println ("\(paddedUser) \(paddedAge)")
}

println ("\n\(merged.count) users")
println ("average age: \(totalAge / Double(merged.count))")
```

The output of our program looks like this:

```
brenda      24
james       41
ryan        28
sarah       19
xavier      32

5 users
average age: 28.8
```

If you've followed along, you should have a good sense for some of the language's capabilities. Already, you've been exposed to comments, arrays and dictionaries, various loop types, type conversion, function calls, extensions, string interpolation, and console output.

The remainder of this book will take you on a tour of these topics and all of the major aspects of the Swift language. Generally, the intention is to cover basic features before more advanced features, but at times it is necessary to dip into advanced topics early on. When this happens, we'll try to warn you in advance and give you a pointer to where you can find more coverage.

Finally, note that this book is about the Swift language, not about iOS or OS X development. O'Reilly has some excellent titles that cover using Swift in those broader contexts, but the examples and discussion you'll find here are deliberately limited to pure Swift as much as possible.

Basic Language Features

Before we delve into the specifics of the language such as data types or program flow, let's take a look at some of the more general aspects of Swift source code.

Comments

Swift supports C-style comments. Comments that extend to the end of the current line begin at a double forward-slash, as illustrated here:

```
// this is a comment
println ("Hello, world")  // really?
```

For multiline comments, you enclose them between a forward-slash followed by an asterisk at the beginning and end them with an asterisk followed by a forward-slash, as shown in the following:

```
/*you could be excused when looking at this comment
for thinking that it was written in C! */
```

Unlike C, Swift supports multiline comment nesting. Swift treats the following as a nested comment block, whereas traditional C compilers will report an error at the last */:

```
/*
/* Original comment here */
*/
```

Multiline comment nesting makes it possible for you to define blocks of commented code using the /* and */ comment markers without having to first check whether an inner multiline comment block exists.

Semicolons

Semicolons in Swift are only required when you need to separate multiple statements on a single line. They are not required at the end of a statement if that is the last statement on the line (but it is not an error to use them):

```
var a = 45;     // semicolons are optional
var b = 55
```

Whitespace

Swift uses whitespaces to separate tokens; otherwise, it ignores them. Whitespaces include spaces, tabs, line feeds, carriage returns, vertical and horizontal tabs, and the null character.

Because whitespace is ignored, you can use line breaks to split long lines at token boundaries. Thus, the following two statements are equivalent:

```
var a = 45

var a
=
45
```

There is no formal way to split a long string over multiple lines as there is in C or Objective-C, but strings can be concatenated by using the + operator. So, you could split a long string like this:

```
let longstr = "Hello there this is a very " +
              "long string split over two lines"
```

Importing Code from Other Modules

In C-like languages, the usual way to use code from other parts of a project or from libraries or frameworks is by using the #include directive. When placed in a source file, this directive instructs the compiler to read a header file into the compilation process.

The header file declares what classes, methods, functions, and external variables are provided by the external code, and are therefore valid to call or access in the source file that hosts the #include directive. The feature provided by the code, or links to it, are linked into the executable file at the last stage of the compilation process by a program called a *linker*.

Swift does away with header files and the need to include them. Instead, Swift uses the `import` command, which imports the definitions made available by another module.

The basic syntax is as follows:

```
import ModuleName
import Cocoa
```

Used in this way, everything that `ModuleName` makes public is imported.

If a module provides submodules, you can import a specific submodule, with this syntax:

```
import ModuleName.SubmoduleName
import Foundation.NSDate
```

If you only want to import a single feature from a module, use this syntax:

```
import Feature ModuleName.SymbolName
import func Darwin.sqrt
```

This last directive imports just the `sqrt` function from the `Darwin` module. `Feature` describes the type of the entity to be imported; the type can be one of the following: `var`, `func`, `class`, `struct`, `enum`, `protocol`, or `typealias` (all of which are described throughout the remainder of this book).

You can import most of the standard OS X and iOS frameworks into a Swift project, including, for example, AppKit, Cocoa, CoreData, Darwin, Foundation, UIKit, and WebKit. Refer to Apple's documentation on OS X and iOS for more information on these and other frameworks at *https:// developer.apple.com*.

In most applications, you'll only need to import Cocoa (for OS X applications) or UIKit (for iOS applications), because they in turn import most other modules that are normally required for these application types.

If you are using the Xcode editor, you can see what additional submodules these modules import or make available by hold-

---

ing down Command-Option and simultaneously clicking the module name in the line that imports that module. (As of this writing, this feature does not work for all modules and can generate errors).

Types

Swift supports the standard data types that you would expect in a modern programming language, which you can see listed in Table 1.

Table 1. Supported data types in Swift

Data Type	Description
Bool	Boolean value (true, false)
Int	Signed integer value
UInt	Unsigned integer value
Double	Double-precision (64-bit) floating-point value
Float	Single-precision (32-bit) floating-point value
Character	A single Unicode character
String	An ordered collection of Characters

Specific Integer Types

Int and UInt are 32- or 64-bit values, as determined by the underlying platform. Swift also supports integer types of specific size (and hence numeric range). Table 2 shows the range of values for each type.

Table 2. Specific integer types and their value ranges

Name	Type	Range
Int8	Signed 8-bit integer	−128 to 127
UInt8	Unsigned 8-bit integer	0 to 255
Int16	Signed 16-bit integer	−32,768 to 32,767

Name	Type	Range
UInt16	Unsigned 16-bit integer	0 to 65,535
Int32	Signed 32-bit integer	−2,147,483,648 to 2,147,483,647
UInt32	Unsigned 32-bit integer	0 to 4,294,967,295
Int64	Signed 64-bit integer	-2^{63} to $2^{63}-1$
UInt64	Unsigned 64-bit integer	0 to $2^{64}-1$

You can determine the maximum and minimum values that can be stored by each integer type by using the max and min properties, as demonstrated in the following example:

```
UInt8.max    // returns 255
Int16.min    // returns -32768
```

Numeric Literals

Numeric literals can be expressed in decimal, binary, octal, or hexadecimal, as presented in Table 3.

Table 3. Expressing numeric literals

Prefix	Base	Example(s)
None	Decimal	17, 1024, 2.767, 2.5e2
0b	Binary	0b10001011
0o	Octal	0o213
0x	Hexadecimal	0x8C, 0x4.8p2

When using numeric literals, also note the following:

- Floating-point literals may be followed by an optional exponent, which is expressed with an e for decimal floating-point literals, or a p for hexadecimal floating-point literals, and which is in turn followed by the exponent itself, in decimal. For example, e3 represents a decimal exponent that multiplies the mantissa by 10^3, and p4 represents a hexadecimal exponent that multiplies the mantissa by 2^4. Examples include `2.7e4`, which equates to 2.7×10^4, and `0x10.4p2`, which equates to $0x10.4 \times 2^2$ (the decimal equivalent being 16.25×2^2).

- To be inferred as a floating-point value, a literal without an exponent must have a decimal point with digits on either side. The presence of an exponent removes the requirement for a decimal point if it is not needed (e.g., `5e2` evaluates to 5.0×10^2).

- Numeric literals can include underscores (but not commas) to aid readability. `1_000_000` and `1_00_00_00` are the same as `1000000`.

- Floating-point literals are treated as `Double` values, unless they are used in a `Float` context.

Character and String Literals

Character literals are single characters surrounded by double-quotes (unlike C-based languages, in which single quotes are used), as shown here:

```
"A", "B", "!"
```

String literals are character sequences surrounded by double-quotes:

```
"Hello, World"
```

The compiler cannot distinguish between a Character literal and a single-character String literal. Literals enclosed in double-quotes are treated by the compiler as Strings, unless they appear in a Character context, such as in assignment:

```
let someChar: Character = "C"
// "C" is treated as a character literal
var c: Character
c = "A"
// "A" is treated as a character literal
```

Type Aliases

The `typealias` keyword defines an alternative name for an existing type. The following example equates the identifier `Byte` with the type `UInt8`:

```
typealias Byte = UInt8
```

After this declaration, `Byte` can then be used as a type anywhere that `UInt8` can be used, such as in the following example:

```
var b: Byte = 64
```

See also the sections "Tuples" on page 26 and "Protocols" on page 131 for examples of type aliases.

Nested Types

Swift supports the definition of types within types, as in this example:

```
class A
{
    class B
    {
        var i = 0
    }
    var j = B()
    var k = 0
}
```

NOTE

The examples shown here draw on content covered later in the text, including *variables* (see "Variables and Constants" on page 21), *classes* (see "Classes" on page 80), and *enumerations* (see "Enumerations" on page 112).

Although you can use such nested definitions to provide utility classes, structures, or enumerations to support the implementation of the outer class, the nested type definitions are visible outside the class as well. For the preceding definition, we can create instances of A and B as follows:

```
var a = A()
var b = A.B()
a.j.i = 2
b.i = 5
```

If a class contains a nested enumeration, as follows:

```
class A
{
    enum TravelClass
    {
        case First, Business, Economy
    }

    // rest of class definition
}
```

then the enumeration can be accessed outside the class by specifying the "path" to the enumeration values, as follows:

```
var t = A.TravelClass.First
```

Other Types

In addition to the types already discussed, you can use many other Swift language elements in a type context, or they can behave as types. These include classes, structures, enumerations, functions, and protocols. These topics are covered in later sections of this book.

Variables and Constants

Variables and *constants* must be declared before you use them.

You declare variables by using the var keyword, followed by the variable's name, a colon, and then its type, as demonstrated here:

```
var name: Type
var a: Int
var s: String
var c: Character
```

You can assign values to variables at the same time that you declare them:

```
var a: Int = 45
var s: String = "Frodo"
```

Swift uses *type inferencing*, which means that you don't need to specify a variable's type if you assign that variable a value when you declare it:

```
var a = 45
var b = 23.0, s = "Strings too"
```

You declare constants by using the `let` keyword. They look like variables in the way that they are created and used, but they are *immutable*—meaning they cannot be changed. Because a constant cannot be changed, it must be assigned a value when it is declared (the exception is for *constant properties* in classes and structures, which can have their value assigned during initialization—see "Classes" on page 80 and "Structures" on page 108 for more information:

```
let name: Type = expr
let b: Float = 23.1
let t: String = "Bilbo"
```

As with variables, the type of a constant will be inferred from the value you assign to it, so in most circumstances, you do not need to specify the type:

```
let b = 23.1
let t = "Bilbo"
```

You can declare the type explicitly for circumstances in which the inferred type is not desired. This is useful when you want to declare a `Character` type where `String` might otherwise be inferred, or a `Float` type where a `Double` might be inferred, as illustrated here:

```
let c: Character = "A"
// "A" is otherwise inferred to be a String
let f: Float = 3.14159
// 3.14149 is otherwise inferred to be a Double
```

The names of variables and constants can contain most Unicode and other characters. They cannot begin with a number.

Some keywords are reserved for specific language features, and you cannot use them as identifiers for variables and constants. Examples include `class`, `func`, `let`, `var`, and so on. However, if you enclose a keyword with backticks, you can use it as an identifier, like this:

```
var func = 4        // not allowed - func is reserved
var `func` = 4      // allowed
```

Despite this, you should be wary of using backticks as a means of using keywords as identifiers. A best practice is to avoid using reserved keywords at all.

Computed Variables

A *computed variable* is not a variable in the usual sense—it is not a value that is stored in memory and read whenever it is referenced in an expression or during assignment. Instead, computed variables are functions that look like variables.

A computed variable contains two functions: a *getter* (identified with the keyword `get`, which returns the computed value) and a *setter* (identified with the keyword `set`, which might initialize the conditions that affect the value returned by the getter). The declaration looks as follows:

```
var variableName: someType
{
    get
    {
        // code that computes and returns
        // a value of someType
    }
    set(valueName)
    {
        // code that sets up conditions
        // using valueName
    }
}
```

The *valueName* is optional; you use it inside the code that implements the setter to refer to the value passed into the set method. If you omit it, the parameter can be referred to using the default name of newValue.

The setter is optional, and for most practical uses, you would not use it. If you don't use the setter, the get clause is not required, and all that is required is code to compute and return a value.

```
var variableName: someType
{
    // code that computes and returns a value
}
```

When a computed variable is defined, it is used exactly like any other variable. If its name is used in an expression, the getter is called. If it is assigned a value, the setter is called:

```
var badPi: Float
{
    return 22.0/7.0
}

let radius=1.5
let circumference = 2.0 * badPi * radius
```

As global or local variables, computed variables would appear to be of limited use, but the same syntax can also be used for properties in structures and classes. In this context, as *computed properties*, the feature becomes more useful. For more information about computed properties, see the section "Properties" on page 84 later in this book.

Variable Observers

Variable observers are functions (or methods) that you can attach to variables and that are called when the value of the variable is about to change (identified with the willSet keyword) or after it has changed (identified with the didSet keyword). The declaration looks as follows:

```
var variableName: someType = expression
{
    willSet(valueName)
    {
        // code called before the value is changed
    }
    didSet(valueName)
    {
        // code called after the value is changed
    }
}
```

When variable observers are used with global and local variables, the type annotation is required, as is the expression used to initialize the variable.

Both *valueName* identifiers (and their enclosing parentheses) are optional.

The willSet function is called immediately before the value of the variable is about to be changed. The new value is visible inside willSet as either *valueName* or newValue if *valueName* was not specified. The function is unable to prevent the assignment from happening and unable to change the value that will be stored in the variable.

The didSet function is called immediately after the value of the variable has been changed (except for after the initial assignment). The old value of the variable is visible inside didSet as either *valueName* or oldValue if *valueName* was not specified:

```
var watcher: Int = 0
{
    willSet
    {
        println("watcher will be changed to \(newValue)")
    }
    didSet
    {
        println("watcher was changed from \(oldValue)")
    }
}
```

The didSet function can modify the value of the observed variable without willSet or didSet being called recursively, so you can use didSet to act as a guard or validator of values stored in the variable. Here is an example of using didSet to ensure that an integer variable can only have an even value:

```
var onlyEven: Int = 0
{
    didSet
    {
        if ((onlyEven & 1) == 1) { onlyEven++ }
    }
}
```

It is not necessary to define both didSet and willSet functions if only one of them is required.

You can use the same syntax that is used for variable observers for properties in structures and classes, creating *property observers*. See the section "Properties" on page 84 for more details.

Tuples

A *tuple* is a group of values that you can treat as a single entity. Tuples are enclosed in parentheses, with each element separated by a comma. Table 4 provides a few examples.

Table 4. Tuple examples

Tuple	Description
(4, 5)	A tuple with two integer parts
(2.0, 4)	A tuple with a floating-point part, and an integer part
("Hello", 2, 1)	A tuple with a string part, and two integer parts

The collection of types of each component of the tuple, in order, is considered to be the *type* of tuple.

The type of each tuple in Table 4 is as follows:

```
(Int, Int)
(Float, Int)
(String, Int, Int)
```

You can store a tuple in a variable or constant of that tuple's type, or pass it to or from functions for which that tuple's type is acceptable.

NOTE

Although they are useful for storing temporary or related values in a single container, tuples are not an appropriate method for storing structured, complex, or persistent data. For such cases, consider using dictionaries, classes, or structures, instead.

Tuple Variables and Constants

To create a variable or constant that stores a tuple, you list the tuple's component types inside parentheses where you would usually specify the type, as shown in the following:

```
var a: (String, Int) = ("Age", 6)
let fullName: (String, String) = ("Bill", "Jackson")
```

Because Swift uses type inferencing, the tuple type can be inferred if the variable or constant is initialized when it is declared. In this example, there is no need to specify that the tuple's type is (String, Int, String), because it is inferred by the compiler:

```
var loco = ("Flying Scotsman", 4472, "4-6-2")
```

Extracting Tuple Components

Much like arrays, you can access tuple components by position, with the first component having an index of 0:

```
var loco = ("Flying Scotsman", 4472, "4-6-2")
let name = loco.0          // assigns "Flying Scotsman"
let number = loco.1        // assigns 4472
```

Naming Tuple Components

You can name tuple components and then access them by those names. This example names the first component of the tuple *name*, and the second component *age*:

```
var person: (name: String, age: Int)
person.name = "Fred"
person.age = 21
let c = person.age

let result = (errCode: 56, errMessage:"file not found")
var s = result.errMessage
// s is now the string "file not found"
```

Using Type Aliases with Tuples

You can use type aliases to associate a type identifier with a tuple type, and that alias can then be used to create new instances of that tuple type:

```
typealias locoDetail =
    (name: String, number: Int, configuration: String)
var thomas: locoDetail = ("Thomas", 1, "0-6-0")
```

Or a function could return a tuple of that type (see also "Functions" on page 51), as demonstrated here:

```
func getNextLoco() -> locoDetail
{
    // do something then return a value of type locoDetail
}
```

Type inferencing works with type aliases, so in

```
var anEngine = getNextLoco()
```

the variable anEngine will also be of type locoDetail.

Tuples as Return Types

Tuples are a convenient way to return more than one value from a function or method call.

Consider a function that, on each successive call, returns the next line of text from a file. At some point, the end of the file

---

will be reached, and this needs to be communicated to the caller. The end-of-file state needs to be returned separately to the line of text itself, and this is a natural fit for a tuple:

```swift
func readLine () -> (Bool, String)
{
    ...
}
```

The function could even name the tuple parameters, as is done here:

```swift
func readLine () -> (eof: Bool, readLine: String)
{
    ...
}
```

Using tuples in this way produces a more natural expression and avoids more opaque techniques to test if the end-of-file was reached.

Operators

Operators are symbols that represent some operation to be applied to values (usually expressed as literals, variables, constants, or expressions). Examples of well-known operators include the plus sign (+), which normally represents addition (or, in the case of strings, concatenation), and the minus sign (–), which represents subtraction.

Operators are often characterized as *unary* (which operate on a single value), *binary* (which operate on two values), or *ternary* (which operate on three values).

The Swift language supports *operator overloading*, so it is important to remember that the actual operation performed by an operator will be determined by the type of data to which it is applied. The descriptions that follow relate to the default behavior. (See also "Operator Overloading" on page 155.)

No Implicit Type Conversion

Before considering the specific operators supported by Swift, you should note that Swift does not do implicit type conversion. This means that the following will not compile, because the operands f and i are of different types (one is a Double, one is an Int):

```
var i = 2
var f = 45.0
let result = (f / i) // error
```

Unlike C-based languages, Swift will not do implicit type conversion in expressions—you must explicitly convert operands to the desired type. For numeric types, that means treating the type as a function, and the operand to be converted as its argument:

```
let result = (f / Double(i))
```

It is also important to note that Swift's type inference rules will treat a floating-point literal as a Double, unless it is used to initialize a variable of type Float. In the preceding example, f is inferred to be a Double, not a Float, so i must be cast to a Double.

Arithmetic Operators

The standard binary arithmetic operators in Swift are the same as in other languages:

+

Addition (or string concatenation, if both operands are strings)

-

Subtraction

*

Multiplication

/

Division

`++`

Pre or post-increment

`--`

Pre- or post-decrement

As with C, these last two unary operators will increment or decrement a variable of Int, Float, or Double type. They also return a value. When you use them as a prefix (the operator appears to the left of the operand), they return the new (incremented) value. When you use them as a postfix (the operator appears to the right of the operand), they return the original (pre-increment/pre-decrement) value.

Bitwise Operators

The following operators are used with integer data types and permit bit-level manipulation:

`~ (~A)`

Bitwise NOT; inverts all bits in a number

`& (A & B)`

Bitwise AND of A and B

`| (A | B)`

Bitwise OR of A and B

`^ (A ^ B)`

Bitwise XOR of A and B

`<< (A << B)`

Bitwise left-shift of A by B bits

`>> (A >> B)`

Bitwise right-shift of A by B bits

When the left operand is an unsigned type, the left-shift and right-shift operators always shift in new bit values of zero.

When the left operand is a signed type, the left-shift and right-shift operators preserve the sign bit at all times. The left-shift operator always shifts in new bit values of zero, whereas the right-shift operator always shifts in new bits with the same value as the sign bit.

Assignment Operators

Other than the regular assignment operator (=), all of the other operators described here are *compound* assignment operators (i.e., they combine another operation, such as addition or subtraction, with an assignment):

`=`

Assignment

`+=`

Add and assign (a += n is equivalent to a = a + n)

`-=`

Subtract and assign (a -= n is equivalent to a = a - n)

`*=`

Multiply and assign (a *= n is equivalent to a = a * n)

`/=`

Divide and assign (a /= n is equivalent to a = a / n)

`%=`

Remainder and assign (a %= n is equivalent to a = a % n)

`<<=`

Bitwise left-shift and assign (a <<= n is equivalent to a = a << n)

`>>=`

Bitwise right-shift and assign (a >>= n is equivalent to a = a >> n)

`&=`

Bitwise AND and assign (`a &= n` is equivalent to `a = a & n`)

`|=`

Bitwise OR and assign (`a |= n` is equivalent to `a = a | n`)

`^=`

Bitwise XOR and assign (`a ^= n` is equivalent to `a = a ^ n`)

NOTE

Unlike C-based languages, assignment operators do not return a value. This prevents a potentially serious error whereby you accidentally type an `=` operator in an `if` statement when you meant to use `==` and end up with code that makes an assignment instead of testing a condition.

Comparison Operators

The *comparison operators* return a Boolean value that represents whether the comparison is true or false. *Equality* refers to whether the left and right operands have the same value. *Identicality* refers to whether the operands reference the same object:

`== (A == B)`

Test equality (same values)

`!= (A != B)`

Test inequality

`=== (A === B)`

Test identitcality (same objects)

`!== (A !== B)`

Test unidentitcality

`< (A < B)`

Test less than

`<= (A <= B)`

Test less than or equal to

`> (A > B)`

Test greater than

`>= (A >= B)`

Test greater than or equal to

`~= (A ~= B)`

Pattern match

Logical Operators

In Swift, non-Boolean values (such as `Int`) cannot be silently cast to Boolean values. These operators can only be used on `Bool` values:

`! (!A)`

Logical NOT; returns the logical opposite of the operand

`&& (A && B)`

Logical AND; returns true if both operands are true

`|| (A || B)`

Logical OR; returns true if either operands is true

Overflow Operators

The *overflow operators* only accept integer operands; they do not cause an error if an arithmetic overflow occurs:

`&+`

Overflow addition

`&-`

Overflow subtraction

`&*`

Overflow multiplication

`&/`

Overflow division (division by 0 returns 0)

`&%`

Overflow remainder (division by 0 returns 0)

Type Casting Operators

is

> Checks whether an instance is of a specific subclass type, or an instance conforms to a protocol.

as

> Forcibly downcasts an instance reference to a specific subclass type, or an instance reference to a specific protocol type. Causes a runtime error if the downcast fails.

as?

> Optionally downcasts an instance reference to a specific subclass type, or an instance reference to a specific protocol type. Returns an optional value if nil of the downcast fails.

See also the sections "Checking and Casting Types" on page 127, and "Protocols" on page 131 later in the book.

Range Operators

The *closed range operator* (x...y) represents all integer values starting at x and ending at y. x must be less than or equal to y. This operator can be used in a loop, as in the following:

```
for i in 1...5
{
    // i will successively take values from 1 through 5
}
```

The *half-open range operator* (x..<y) represents all integer values starting at x and ending at y – 1. The value for x must be less than or equal to y – 1:

```
for i in 0..<5
{
    // i will successively take values from 0 through 4
}
```

See also the section "Ranges, Intervals, and Strides" on page 160 for more information.

Ternary Conditional Operator

Swift's *ternary conditional operator* performs the same function as its syntactic counterpart in C. The basic format is as follows:

```
expr1 ? expr2 : expr3
```

If *expr1* evaluates to true, the operator returns *expr2*. Otherwise, it returns *expr3*.

This operator provides a shorthand equivalent of:

```
var a: Int
if (someCondition)
{
    a = 6
}
else
{
    a = 9
}
```

reducing it to the following:

```
var a: Int = someCondition ? 6 : 9
```

Operator Precedence

When evaluating expressions that consist of more than a single operator, and where there are no parentheses to control evaluation order, Swift uses a simple set of rules to determine the order of evaluation. Let's take a look at the following expression:

```
4 * 5 + 3
```

By convention, we treat the multiplication as a higher priority operator than the addition, and so the expression is evaluated to 23, and not 32.

Swift classifies the built-in operators as belonging to one of eleven groups and uses numeric *precedence* levels to determine overall evaluation order. Operators at higher levels are evaluated before operators at lower levels.

In addition, when two operators with the same precedence level are being evaluated, Swift uses predefined *associativity* values to determine which to evaluate first. Associativity values are declared as none, left, and right:

- A value of left means the lefthand subexpression will be evaluated first.

- A value of right means the righthand subexpression will be evaluated first.

- A value of none means that operators at this precedence level cannot be adjacent to each other.

Table 5 shows the precedence and associativity values for the built-in operators.

Table 5. Built-in operator precedence and associativity values

Precedence	Associativity	Operators
160	None	<<, >>
150	Left	*, /, %, &*, &/, &%, &
140	Left	+, -, &+, &-, |, ^
135	None	..<, ...
132	None	is, as
130	None	<, <=, >, >=, ==, !=, ===, !==, ~=
120	Left	&&
110	Left	||
110	Right	??
100	Right	? : (ternary conditional)
90	Right	=, *=, /=, %=, +=, -=, <<=, >=, &=, ^=, |=, &&=, ||=

Using Table 5, we can see that in

```
4 << 5 * 4
```

the left-shift operator (<<) will be evaluated first because it has a higher precedence level than the multiply operator (*).

For an expression in which operands have the same precedence, the associativity values are applied. Consider this expression:

```
4 + 3 &- 88
```

Both the addition operator (+) and the overflow subtraction operator (&-) are precedence level 150, but they are left associative, which means that the lefthand subexpression is evaluated first, causing the expression to be interpreted as follows:

```
(4 + 3) &- 88
```

Strings and Characters

A String is an ordered collection of Characters. The Character type is Unicode-compliant, so Strings are also fully Unicode-compliant.

Empty string and character variables are declared as follows:

```
var astring: String
var achar: Character
```

Or they can be initialized by using a string literal value:

```
var astring: String = "Hello"
var achar: Character = "A"
```

Like String literals, Character literals are enclosed in double-quotes. (Swift does not permit characters to be enclosed in single-quotes, which might confuse C programmers.)

Because Swift can infer types, it is not necessary to include the String keyword when assigning a value, so you can also write the previous examples as follows:

```
var astring = "Hello"
var achar: Character = "A"
```

You can concatenate String types by using the + operator to create a new String:

```
let newString = "Hello" + " Bill"
```

Or you can append a String to an existing String by using the += operator:

```
var welcome = "Hello"
welcome += " there"
```

Strings are a *value type* and are copied when assigned or passed to a function or method (unlike NSStrings, which are passed by *reference*).

String Properties

You can use the following features to check string length and get alternate views of the string in different character formats:

someString.isEmpty

> Boolean; true, if the string contains no characters.

countElements(someString)

> Returns the number of characters in the string. Because Swift strings are Unicode-compliant, the number of characters might not be the same as the length of the string in bytes.

someString.utf8

> A view of the string in UTF-8 format (of type String.UTF8View), for iterating over the string's characters in 8-bit format.

someString.utf16

> A view of the string in UTF-16 format (of type String.UTF16View), for iterating over the string's characters in 16-bit format.

someString.unicodeScalars

> A view of the string in UnicodeScalar format (of type UnicodeScalarView), for iterating over the string's characters in UnicodeScalar format.

Comparing Strings

You can compare strings and substrings by using the following comparison operators and methods:

==
> Returns true if two strings contain the same sequence of characters.

!=
> Returns true if two strings contain different sequences of characters.

<
> Returns true if the string to the left of the operator sorts lexically before the string to the right of the operator.

<=
> Returns true if the string to the left of the operator sorts lexically before or is equal to the string to the right of the operator.

>
> Returns true if the string to the left of the operator sorts lexically after the string to the right of the operator.

>=
> Returns true if the string to the left of the operator sorts lexically after or is equal to the string to the right of the operator.

someString.hasPrefix(*prefixString*)
> Returns true if the sequence of characters in *prefix String* matches the start of *someString*.

someString.hasSuffix(*suffixString*)
> Returns true if the sequence of characters in *suffix String* matches the end of *someString*.

Escaped Characters in Strings

To use certain special characters in string literals, use a backslash escape sequence:

`\0`

Null character

`\\`

Backslash

`\t`

Tab

`\n`

Line feed

`\r`

Carriage return

`\"`

Double quote

`\'`

Single quote

`\u{n}`

Arbitrary Unicode scalar; *n* is from 1 to 8 hex digits

String Interpolation

Expressions can be evaluated and the result substituted in a string literal using the escape sequence:

```
\(expr)
```

For example:

```
let costOfMeal = 56.52
let advice = "Consider tipping around \(costOfMeal * 0.20)"
```

String interpolation is not restricted to numeric values:

```
let a = "Hi"
let b = "there"
let c = "\(a) \(b)"        // c is now "Hi there"
```

Arrays

An array is a collection of items of the same type, be it a simple type (such as Int, Double, or String) or a more complex type (such as a class or structure). You access elements in an array by their position in the collection using a subscript syntax. This example assigns the sixth element in the array to the constant v (because array elements start at 0):

```
let v = vertex[5]
```

The type of an array is formally specified as Array<Type>, although the more frequently used shorthand equivalent is [Type]. Thus, if you see the term [String], you can conclude that it means an array of type String.

You declare arrays in a similar way to variables and constants. You create empty arrays as follows:

```
var arrayName = [Type]()
var daysPerWeek = [String]()
```

You can declare arrays with a specified number of pre-initialized entries:

```
var vertex = [Double](count: 3, repeatedValue: 0.0)
```

Or you can initialize them by using an *array literal*:

```
var locos: [String] = ["Puffing Billy", "Thomas"]
let daysPerMonth: [Int] =
    [31, 28, 31, 30, 31, 30, 31, 31, 30, 31, 31, 31]
let primes = [1, 3, 5, 7, 11]
```

You can also use the + operator to create an array that combines existing arrays of the same type, as shown here:

```
let vowels = ["A", "E", "I", "O", "U"]
let consonants = ["B", "C", "D", "F", "G", "H", "J", …]
var allLetters = vowels + consonants
```

Here are some more characteristics of arrays in Swift:

- Arrays declared by using var are *mutable*, whereas arrays declared by using let are *immutable*.

- An array's type does not need to be specified if it is initialized from an array literal, because the type can be inferred.

- All entries in an array must be of the same type (unlike Objective-C's NSArray class, which can store a collection of arbitrary objects).

- Arrays are a *value type* and are copied when assigned or passed to a function or method (unlike NSArray, which is passed by *reference*).

Accessing Array Elements

You access array elements by using C-style subscript syntax. Remember, the first element in an array has an index of 0:

```
let days = daysPerMonth[5]
```

It is also possible to access a subset of elements at one time by using a *range*. This operation returns a new array:

```
let newArray = oldArray[5...7]
```

If you attempt to access an element beyond the end of the array, a runtime error will occur.

arrayName.first
> Returns the first element in the array.

arrayName.last
> Returns the last element in the array.

Array Properties

To examine the properties of an array, use the following features:

arrayName.capacity
> Integer: the number of elements the array can store without it being relocated in memory.

arrayName.count

   Integer: the number of elements in the array.

arrayName.isEmpty

   Boolean: true, if the array has no elements.

Modifying a Mutable Array

You can modify mutable arrays in the following ways:

arrayName.append(*value*)

   Adds a new element to the end of the array.

arrayName += *array*

   Appends (copies) one array to the end of another.

arrayName[*n*] = *value*

   Store a value in element *n*, replacing the existing value there. A runtime error will occur if you attempt to write beyond the end of the array. To "grow" the array (i.e., add more entries), use the append method.

arrayName[*range*] = *array*

   Replace a range of elements with an array of the same type. Ranges are specified as [*start...end*]. All elements from [start] to [end] are removed and replaced with copies of the elements in array. The size of the range does not have to be the same as the size of the array replacing it; the array will expand or contract to hold the replacement.

arrayName.insert(*value*, atIndex: *n*)

   Insert a new value in front of element *n*.

arrayName.removeAll(keepCapacity: *Bool*)

   Removes all elements from the array. The keepCapacity argument is optional and defaults to false. If set to true, the capacity of the array will remain unchanged.

arrayName.removeAtIndex(*n*)

   Remove (and return) element *n* from the array.

```
arrayName.removeLast()
```
Removes (and returns) the last element of the array.
```
arrayName.reserveCapacity(n)
```
Ensures that the array has sufficient capacity to store *n* elements without further relocation, by relocating it if necessary.
```
arrayName.sort
```
Sorts the elements of the array. Used with a closure to define how two elements sort with respect to each other (e.g., names.sort { $0<$1 }). (See also the section "Closures" on page 57.)

Iterating Over Arrays

To iterate over all elements in an array, you use a for-in loop:

```
for item in arrayName
{
    …
}
```

Let's take a closer look at how this works:

- The code in the braces is executed once for each item in the array.

- For each execution, *item* takes on the value of the next element, starting at the first element.

- *item* is a constant—although its value changes with each iteration, it cannot be modified in the loop.

To use both the position and value of items from the array, use the enumerate function, as shown here:

```
for (index, item) in enumerate(arrayName)
{
    …
}
```

The enumerate() function returns a tuple consisting of the integer index and value of each item in the array.

Array Algorithms

Most of the algorithms that you can apply to arrays use *closures*. These are anonymous functions that perform some operation on one or two elements of the array (such as a transform, or comparison). See the section "Closures" on page 57 for more information.

The examples that follow are demonstrated using this array of strings:

```
var names = ["John", "Zoe", "Laura", "albert", "Allen"]
```

arrayName.filter()

Returns a new array that contains only the elements that match some condition, which is defined by using a closure. This example filters names longer than four characters:

```
names.filter { countElements($0) > 4 }
// returns ["Laura", "albert", "Allen"]
```

arrayName.map()

Returns a new array in which each element has been transformed by a mapping function, which is defined by using a closure. This example returns an array in which any string from the original array that does not start with an uppercase "A" is prefixed with an asterisk (*):

```
names.filter { $0.hasPrefix("A") ? $0 : "*" + $0 }
// returns:
// ["*John", "*Zoe", "*Laura", "*albert", "Allen"]
```

arrayName.reduce()

Returns a single value (of the type stored in the array) derived by recursively applying a reduction filter (defined by using a closure) to each element of the array and the output of the previous recursion. This example seeds the recursion with an empty string ($0) and concatenates each element of the array ($1) to the output of the previous recursion ($0):

```
names.reduce("") { $0 + $1 }
// returns "JohnZoeLauraalbertAllen"
```

`arrayName.reverse()`

> Returns a new array that contains the elements of *array Name* in reverse order, as shown here:

```
names.reverse()
// returns ["Allen", "albert", "Laura", "Zoe", "John"]
```

`arrayName.sorted()`

> Returns a new array that contains the elements of *array Name* in sorted order. Used with a closure to define how two elements sort with respect to each other. For example:

```
names.sorted { $0<$1 }
// returns ["Allen", "John", "Laura", "Zoe", "albert"]
```

Dictionaries

Much like arrays, dictionaries store a collection of values, but whereas array elements are referenced via position, dictionary elements are referenced via unique *keys*.

A dictionary's type is formally specified as Dictionary<*Key Type*, *ValueType*>, although the preferred shorthand equivalent is [*KeyType*:*ValueType*]. Thus, if you see the term [String:Int], you can assume that it means a dictionary whose key type is String and whose value type is Int.

Dictionaries are declared in a similar way to variables and constants. You can create empty dictionaries like so:

```
var dictionaryName = [Type: Type]()
var cpus = [String: String]()
```

Or you can initialize them upon declaration by using a *dictionary literal*, as demonstrated here:

```
var cpus: [String:String] =
    ["BBC Model B":"6502", "Lisa":"68000", "TRS-80":"Z80"]
```

The type of both the key and the value can be inferred when initialized with a dictionary literal, so we can reduce the previous example to the following:

```
var cpus =
    ["BBC Model B":"6502",  "Lisa":"68000", "TRS-80":"Z80"]
```

If you're not initializing a dictionary with a literal value, you can specify a minimum capacity by using the following:

```
var dictionaryName = [Type: Type](minimumCapacity: Int)
var cpus = [String: String](minimumCapacity: 5)
```

Specifying a minimum capacity could be useful for improving performance of dictionaries that are frequently mutated. Unlike arrays, you cannot determine the capacity of a dictionary, and you cannot reserve additional capacity after creation to improve performance.

Here are some more characteristics of dictionaries in Swift:

- All keys in a dictionary must be of the same type.

- All values in a dictionary must be of the same type.

- The contents of a dictionary are stored in arbitrary order.

- Dictionaries are a *value type* and are copied when assigned or passed to a function or method (unlike NSDictionary, which is passed by *reference*).

Accessing Dictionary Elements

To access dictionary values, you use the key as a subscript, as illustrated here:

```
let cpu = cpus["BBC Model B"]
```

Dictionary Properties

You can use the following features to access various properties of a dictionary:

dictionaryName.isEmpty

Boolean: true, if the dictionary has no elements.

dictionaryName.count

Integer: the number of key-value pairs in the dictionary.

dictionaryName.keys

Returns an array of all keys in the dictionary, which you can use for iterating over the keys in a dictionary (see "Iterating Over Dictionaries" on page 50). The returned keys are in no particular order. To use this in an array context, you must copy it to a new array by using this syntax:

```
let newArrayName = [Type](dictionaryName.keys)
```

dictionaryName.values

Returns an array of all values in the dictionary, which can be used for iterating over the values in a dictionary (see "Iterating Over Dictionaries" on page 50). The returned keys are in no particular order. To use this in an array context, you must copy it to a new array by using the following syntax:

```
let newArrayName = [Type](dictionaryName.values)
```

Modifying a Mutable Dictionary

You can modify mutable dictionaries in the following ways:

dictionaryName[*key*] = *value*

Sets (or updates) the value of the element identified by *key*. To remove this key-value pair from the dictionary, set *value* to nil.

dictionaryName.updateValue(*newValue*, forKey: *key*)

Sets (or updates) the value of the element identified by *key*. Returns the old value as an *optional* (see "Optionals" on page 63) if there was one.

dictionaryName.removeAll(keepCapacity: *Bool*)

Removes all elements from the dictionary. The keepCapacity argument is optional, and defaults to false. If

set to `true`, the capacity of the dictionary will remain
unchanged.

`dictionaryName.removeValueForKey(key)`

Removes a key-value pair from the dictionary identified by `key`. Returns the value that was removed or `nil`
if there was no value for `key`.

Iterating Over Dictionaries

To iterate over all elements in a dictionary, you use a `for-in`
loop, as shown in the following:

```
for (key, value) in dictionaryName
{
    …
}
```

Let's take a closer look at how this works:

- The code inside the braces is executed once for each item
  in the array.

- For each execution, *key* and *value* take on successive key-
  value pairs from the dictionary. Dictionaries are stored in
  arbitrary order.

- *key* and *value* are constant—although their values
  change with each iteration, they cannot be modified in
  the loop.

To iterate over just the keys or values of the dictionary, use the
keys or values property, which returns an unsorted array:

```
for value in dictionaryName.values
{
    …
}

for key in dictionaryName.keys
{
    …
}
```

Functions

You declare functions in Swift by using the `func` keyword, as shown in the following:

```
func functionName(parameters) -> returnType { … body … }
```

Here are some characteristics of, and usage tips for Swift functions:

- Functions can have zero or more parameters.
- If there are no parameters, empty parentheses must still be provided.
- Functions do not have to return a value.
- If the function does not return a value, omit the arrow and *returnType*.

Parameter Types

By default, function parameters are constant (they cannot be modified in the function body). *Variable* parameters are created by preceding them in the function declaration with the `var` keyword, as shown here:

```
func someFunc(var s: someType) -> …
```

You can use the variable *s* as a local, modifiable variable in the function body. Variable parameters are lost after the function returns—you cannot use them to pass values outside the function body.

In-out parameters are created by preceding them in the function declaration with the `inout` keyword, like so:

```
func someFunc(inout i: someType) -> …
```

i becomes an alias for an external variable passed by reference. Modifying *i* inside the function modifies the external variable. Like variable references in C++, you must place an ampersand (&) before a referenced variable's name in a function call:

```
var i: Int = 45
someFunc(&i)
```

Returning Optional Values

A function can return an *optional* value, which is a way to indicate that no valid return value can be provided. Suppose that we were implementing a (pointless!) function to do division. The function definition might start out like this:

```
func division(dividend: Double, divisor: Double) -> Double
{
    return dividend / divisor
}
```

It is possible that the divisor might be zero, which would cause a runtime error. With an optional return value, we can indicate when the result is valid and when it is not. To specify that a return value is optional, follow it with a question mark. Our function thus becomes:

```
func division(dividend: Double, divisor: Double) -> Double?
{
    if (divisor == 0) { return nil }
    return dividend / divisor
}
```

If the divisor is zero, we return a nil value; otherwise, we return the result of the operation.

Because the return value is now an optional, we need to test it before using it. To do that, we use this syntax:

```
var d = division (9.0, 0.0)
if d != nil
{
    // value is valid
    println (d!)
}
else
{
    // value is invalid
}
```

See also the sections "Optionals" on page 63 and "Optional Chaining" on page 66.

Returning Multiple Values by using Tuples

You can have a function return more than one value by using a tuple, such as in the following example:

```
func getRange() -> (lower: Int, upper: Int)
{
    ...
    return (someLowValue, someHighValue)
}
```

Because the tuple members are named in the function declaration in the preceding example, those names can be used to refer to the components after the function call. Thus, you could access the two values like this:

```
let limits = getRange();
for i in limits.lower...limits.upper { ... }
```

The optional tuple return type

For cases in which a tuple is the return type of a function, you might want to indicate that the tuple has no value. Extending the previous getRange() example, it might be the case that no valid range exists, and thus there is nothing to return. This can be managed by using an optional return type for the tuple, which you indicate by following the parentheses around the return type with a question mark, and returning nil (instead of a tuple) if the range is not valid:

```
func getRange() -> (lower: Int, upper: Int)?
{
    if (rangeIsNotValid) { return nil }
    ...
    return (someLowValue, someHighValue)
}
```

For more information, see the section "Optionals" on page 63.

Local and External Parameter Names

Parameter names such as *p1* in this example act as a *local* parameter name that is used inside the function body.

```
func f(p1: Int) { ... }
```

A caller of the function provides a single integer value as the parameter value:

```
let a = f(45)
```

For functions with more than a few parameters, specify *external* parameter names to make clear the role of each parameter. You specify external parameter names as follows:

```
func funcName(externalName internalName: type, …)
func search (string s: String, forString s2: String)
    -> Int { … }
```

The search function thus defined would be called like this:

```
let openDoor =
    search(string: userInput, forString: "open sesame")
```

Where the local and external parameter names can be the same, you can write the name once, and prefix it with #. For example, the following defines forString as both the internal and external name of the second parameter:

```
func search (string s: String,
    # forString: String) -> Int { … }
```

Where external parameter names have been declared, they are not optional and must be used in calls to that function. In addition, external names do not provide an "arbitrary order" feature for parameters. For example, the following would not compile using the previously defined function:

```
let openDoor = search(forString: "open sesame",
    string: userInput)
// compiler error: Argument 'string' must
// precede argument 'forString'
```

Default Parameter Values

To add default values for any parameters, use the following:

```
func search (string s: String,
    forString s2: String = "open sesame") -> Int { … }
```

If the `forString` parameter is omitted in a function call, such as in the example that follows, the default value of "open sesame" will be used for that parameter:

```
let openDoor = search(string: userInput)
```

NOTE

If you provide a default value for a parameter without an external name, Swift will generate an external name that matches the local name.

Variadic Parameters

A *variadic* parameter supports a variable number of input values. You specify a variadic parameter by following the parameter type with an ellipsis (…), as demonstrated here:

```
func sumOfInts(numbers: Int...) -> Int { … }
```

The function would then be called as follows:

```
let total = sumOfInts(2, 3)
let anotherTotal = sumOfInts(5, 9, 11, 13, 22)
```

In the body of the function, the values passed as arguments to the function are available in an array (in this case, called numbers).

When using variatic parameters, you should make note of the following:

- A function can only have one variadic parameter.

- A variadic parameter must appear after all other parameters.

Function Types

A function's type is an expression of the types of its input parameters and its result. For example, for:

```
func sumOfInts(numbers: Int...) -> Int {...}
func search (string s: String, forString s2: String)
    -> Int {...}
func doesNothing() {...}
```

the types are, respectively:

```
(Int...) -> Int
(String, String) -> Int
() -> ()
```

You can use function types in many places where you can use simpler types (such as Int). For example, you can declare a variable or constant to be a function type, as shown here:

```
var generalPurposeFunc: (Int) -> Int
```

You can then assign the variable *generalPurposeFunc* a function of the same type:

```
func addOne (i: Int) -> Int { return i+1 }
func addTwo (i: Int) -> Int { return i+2 }
generalPurposeFunc = addOne
```

That variable can then be used where the function could be used:

```
addOne(4)        // returns 5
generalPurposeFunc(5)    // returns 6
generalPurposeFunc = addTwo
generalPurposeFunc(5)    // returns 7
```

You can pass functions as parameters to other functions, and functions can be returned by other functions. You specify the function type as either the type of the parameter or the type of the returned value. The example that follows defines a function whose only parameter is a function that takes an integer parameter and then returns an integer value. The defined function does not itself return a value at all:

```
func adaptable(inputFunc: (Int)->Int) -> () { ... }
```

The next example defines a function that takes a single integer parameter and then returns a function. The returned function is defined as taking a single integer parameter and returning a single integer parameter:

```
func selectOperation(i: Int) -> (Int)-> Int { … }
```

Closures

Closures are functionally similar to *blocks* in Objective-C and *lambdas* in languages such as Scheme, C#, and Python.

Closures are anonymous functions that can be passed as arguments to other functions (known as *higher-order functions*) or returned by other functions. They can refer to variables and parameters of the scope in which they are defined (sometimes called *outer variables*). In doing so, they are said to capture or *close over* those values.

You typically define a closure through a *closure expression*, which takes the following format:

```
{
    (parameters) -> returnType in
        statements
}
```

To gain a better understanding of where closures can be useful, consider the operation of sorting arrays. The C standard library provides a number of sorting functions, one of which is qsort(), which takes as a parameter a pointer to a comparison function. This comparison function, defined by the caller, takes as parameters two pointers to two entities that are to be compared. The comparison function returns an integer that is less than, equal to, or greater than zero depending on whether the first entity is less than, equal to, or greater than the second.

A closure is a concise way of providing similar functionality without having to define a named function to do the comparison. Instead, the closure is passed as an inline parameter to the sort function.

The Swift standard library includes a function, sorted(), that creates a sorted copy of an array. You use it as follows:

```
let names = ["John", "Zoe", "Laura", "albert", "Allen"]
let s = sorted(names)
// s is now ["Allen", "John", "Laura", "Zoe", "albert"]
```

Swift knows how to compare built-in types such as Strings, Ints, and Floats; therefore, it can sort arrays of these types into ascending or lexical order. In the preceding example, sorted() applies its default behavior for the String type and sorts lexically ("albert" sorts after "Zoe" because lowercase characters sort lexically after uppercase characters).

There exists another version of sorted() that takes a closure as its second parameter. The closure takes two values (of the same type as the array's content) and must return true if the first value should sort before the second (much like the comparison function required by qsort() described earlier). If the array being sorted contains strings, the closure must be defined as follows:

```
(String, String) -> Bool
```

In other words, the closure must take two String parameters and return a Bool value that indicates whether the first sorts before the second.

This is how you would call sorted() and provide a closure that replicates the behavior of the simpler version already described:

```
let t = sorted(names, { (s1: String, s2: String) ->
    Bool in return s1<s2 } )
```

Because Swift can infer types from context, you can usually omit them. The array is an array of strings, so it follows that the two closure parameters must also be of type String. The closure must return a Bool. Because all of the types can be inferred, they can be omitted. And as there are now no types to specify, you can also omit the parentheses and the arrow. Thus, you can reduce the closure to this:

```
let t = sorted(names, { s1, s2 in return s1<s2 } )
```

For simple closures with a single expression, such as that just demonstrated, you can also omit the return keyword, which reduces the closure further to the following:

```
let t = sorted(names, { s1, s2 in s1<s2 } )
```

To produce a reversed variant of the sort, switch the order of the strings being compared. This effectively returns false if the first value should sort before the second:

```
let u = sorted(names, { s1, s2 in s2<s1 } )
// u is now ["albert", "Zoe", "Laura", "John", "Allen"]
```

Alternatively, reverse the comparison operator, as shown here:

```
let u = sorted(names, { s1, s2 in s1>=s2 } )
// u is now ["albert", "Zoe", "Laura", "John", "Allen"]
```

To sort by string length instead of lexically, modify the comparison operands in the closure to compare the lengths of the two strings being compared:

```
let v = sorted(names,
    { s1, s2 in countElements(s1)<countElements(s2) } )
// v is now ["Zoe", "John", "Laura", "Allen", "albert"]
```

Automatic Argument Names

In the discussion of closures, we defined our own names to refer to each argument required by the closure. For example, when sorting an array of strings, we named the arguments s1 and s2 so that we could refer to them subsequently in the comparison expression:

```
let u = sorted(names, { s1, s2 in s2<s1 } )
```

For simple inline closures, having to first name the arguments just so that you can subsequently refer to them makes the closure longer than it needs to be. For inline closures, Swift assigns *automatic argument names* to each parameter by using a dollar sign followed by a position number ($0, $1, $2, etc.).

Recall from earlier that (for sorting a string array) the closure required by sorted() is defined as follows:

```
(String, String) -> Bool
```

There are two string parameters and Swift aliases their arguments as $0 and $1. Using these aliases means that we don't have to define them ourselves, and the sorted() closure examples reduce further still to this:

```
let t = sorted(names, { $0<$1 } )
let u = sorted(names, { $1<$0 } )
let v = sorted(names,
    { countElements($0)<countElements($1) } )
```

Trailing Closures

When the last (or only) argument provided to a function is a closure, you can write it as a *trailing closure*. Trailing closures are written after the parentheses that wrap the function's arguments:

```
let t = sorted(names) { $0<$1 }
let u = sorted(names) { $1<$0 }
let v = sorted(names)
    { countElements($0)<countElements($1) }
```

If the function has no other arguments than the closure itself, and you're using trailing closure syntax, you can omit the empty parentheses.

Capturing Values

As with any regular function, closures are able to refer to state in the scope in which they are defined (e.g., local variables or constants defined in the same scope). But, similar to functions, closures can be returned by their containing function, which means that a closure could be executed after the values that it refers to have gone out of scope.

This situation does not result in a runtime error. The closure is said to *capture* those values, and extend their lifetime beyond the scope in which they are defined.

In the example that follows, a function (makeTranslator) creates new functions (closures) and returns them as its result. It takes a single parameter (a string) with the local name

greeting. The function that it returns takes a single parameter
(a string) and returns a single parameter (a string):

```
func makeTranslator(greeting: String) -> (String) -> String
{
    return
        {
            (name: String) -> String in
                return (greeting + " " + name)
        }
}
```

The closures that are built by this function capture the
greeting string value and use it later whenever they are executed, even though that value has since gone out of scope.

Here is how you might use this function:

```
var englishWelcome = makeTranslator("Hello")
var germanWelcome = makeTranslator("Guten Tag")
```

After this has been executed, englishWelcome will refer to a closure that takes a single string argument and will return it with
the word "Hello" prepended, whereas germanWelcome will refer
to a closure that takes a single string argument and will return
it with the words "Guten Tag" prepended.

Because englishWelcome and germanWelcome refer to closures,
and closures are functions, we call them in the same manner
that we call any function:

```
englishWelcome ("Bill")
// returns "Hello Bill"
germanWelcome ("Johan")
// returns "Guten Tag Johan"
```

The closures and the values that they have captured will remain
available until the variables that refer to them go out of scope
or are set to new values. For example, if we change the definition of englishWelcome like this:

```
englishWelcome = makeTranslator("G'day")
englishWelcome ("Bruce")
// returns "G'day Bruce"
```

then the storage allocated to the "Hello" version of the closure and its captured values will be released.

Capturing Values by Reference

In the preceding discussion, the value captured (the `greeting` string value) is actually copied when the closure is constructed, because that value is never modified by the closure.

Values that a closure modifies are not copied but are instead captured by *reference*. Here's a revised example that keeps count of the number of times it has been called:

```
func makeTranslator(greeting: String, personNo: String) ->
    (String) -> String
{
    var cnt = 0

    return
    {
      (name: String) -> String in
        cnt++
        return (greeting + " " + name + ", " +
                personNo + " \(cnt)")
    }
}
```

Next, we construct two new closures to make greetings:

```
var germanWelcome = makeTranslator("Guten Tag",
    "Sie sind Nummer")
var aussieWelcome = makeTranslator("G'day", "you're number")
```

And then we call them:

```
germanWelcome ("Johan")
// returns "Guten Tag Johan, Sie sind Nummer 1"
aussieWelcome ("Bruce")
// returns "G'day Bruce, you're number 1"
aussieWelcome ("Kylie")
// returns "G'day Kylie, you're number 2"
```

Each closure stores a reference to `cnt`, which is a local variable in the `makeTranslator()` function. In doing so, they extend the lifetime of that local variable to the lifetime of the closure.

Note that each closure still gets its own instance of cnt because they existed as two different instances, separated by the two executions of makeTranslator.

Optionals

Swift's *optionals* provide a way to indicate that a value exists without usurping some part of the value's set of possible states to do so.

For example, an application might want to record if a piece of string is present in the physical world, and if so, record what the length of that piece of string is. In this example, a negative value (such as –1) could be used to indicate that the string is not present, because such a value could never represent an actual length. This example uses a single store to represent whether the string is present and (only if it is) what its length is.

A similar technique is often used in Objective-C, where objects (or, more precisely, *pointers* to objects) may be nil, indicating that there is no object. Many Objective-C method calls return either (a pointer to) an object or nil if the method call has failed or some other error has occurred.

In Swift, object references are not pointers and may not normally be set to nil, unless they are explicitly declared to be optional values. An example of the syntax for such a declaration is as follows:

```
var str: String?
```

The question mark, which immediately follows the type, declares that the variable str is an optional. Its value might exist or it might not. Not having a value is not the same as str storing an empty string. (When a new optional is created in this way, it's initial value is set to nil).

When a variable has been declared to be optional, it must either be used in places where an optional context for that type is allowed, or it must be unwrapped (see the section "Unwrapping Optionals" on page 64) to reveal the underlying value.

For example, you can assign an optional to another optional without issue, as shown here:

```
var n: String?
n = str
```

However, you cannot assign it to a nonoptional:

```
var r: String
r = str  // will produce a compile-time error
```

Because r is not an optional, the compiler won't allow an optional to be assigned to it.

If an optional's value exists, assign nil to it to remove that value:

```
str = nil
```

Only optionals can be assigned nil in this way. Attempting to assign nil to a nonoptional variable or constant will result in a compile-time error.

Unwrapping Optionals

To access the value stored by an optional, first check if a value exists with the if statement. If it does exist, use the exclamation mark to *force unwrap* the optional and access the raw value it stores, as demonstrated here:

```
if str              // check if the optional has a value
{
    r = str!        // it does - unwrap it and copy it
}
else
{
    // the optional had no value
}
```

Force unwrapping an optional for which no value exists will result in a runtime error.

Implicitly Unwrapped Optionals

In some situations, it might be appropriate to use an optional, even if it will always have a value. For example, an optional created by using `let` cannot be mutated (so it cannot be reset to `nil`), and it must be initialized when it is declared, so it can never not have a value:

```
let constantString: String? = "Hello"
```

Even though its value cannot change, the value must be still unwrapped to use it in a nonoptional context:

```
var mutableString: String
mutableString = constantString    // compile-time error
mutableString = constantString!   // allowed
```

For this and other uses, Swift provides *implicitly unwrapped optionals*, which are defined by using an exclamation mark after the type instead of a question mark. After it is defined, a reference to the optional's value does not need to be unwrapped; it is implicitly unwrapped whenever it is referenced:

```
let constantString: String! = "Hello"
mutableString = constantString
```

This example is contrived, but implicitly unwrapped optionals play a role during class initialization. See the section "Classes" on page 80 for more information.

Optional Binding

Optional binding is a way to test whether an optional has a value, and, if it does, make a scoped nonoptional copy for use inside the if statement. The syntax, which does not read naturally, but is likely to become second nature for seasoned Swift developers, is as follows:

```
if let someConst = someOpt
{
    // someConst is now an unwrapped version of someOpt
    println (someConst)
}
```

Assuming the optional *someOpt* has a value, *someConst* holds a copy of that value inside the braces of the if statement. Because *someConst* is not an optional, its value can be used directly—the unwrapping has been handled in the let statement.

Use var instead of let to create an unwrapped copy of the optional that is mutable. Modifying the value copied in this way does not change the original optional value.

Optional Chaining

When you access an optional, it either has a value or is nil, and you need to test that the value exists before unwrapping it, as in the following example:

```
var s: String?

if s              // check if the optional has a value
{
    var r = s!    // it does - do something with it
}
else
{
    // the optional had no value
}
```

You can use optionals anywhere that a value might or might not exist:

- A property of a class, structure, or enumeration might hold an optional value.

- A method of a class, structure, or enumeration might return an optional value.

- A subscript of a class, structure, or enumeration might return an optional value.

This content appears here as it relates to optionals, but the topic and the examples used to illustrate it also require an understanding of *classes* (see "Classes" on page 80) or *structures* (see "Structures" on page 108) and *subscripts* (see "Subscripts" on page 93).

Optional chaining is a facility by which you can query an optional, or something that depends on an optional having a value, without specifically having to test the optional first. You use optional chaining when accessing class, structure, or enumeration properties, methods, or subscripts using dot-syntax.

Consider this simple example of two classes, in which class A contains an optional reference to an instance of class B:

```
class A
{
    var otherClass: B?
}

class B
{
    var someProperty: Int = 7
    func someMethod()
    {
        println ("someMethod called!")
    }
    subscript (index: Int) -> String
    {
        get { return "getter for [\(index)] called" }
        set {  }
    }
}
```

Now, assume that we have an optional reference to an instance of class A, as in the following example:

```
var a: A?
```

Let's further assume that we want to follow the path from our optional reference a through to someProperty or someMethod()

of class B. Without optional chaining, we would need to check that each optional has a value; if it does (and only if it does), can we descend down to the next level, like this:

```
if a != nil
{
    if a!.otherClass != nil
    {
        println (a!.otherClass!.someProperty)
    }
    else
    {
        println ("no property available")
    }
}
else
{
    println ("no property available")
}
```

This leads to potentially deep conditional tests, which is what optional chaining simplifies. With optional chaining (and let binding), you can reduce the code to the following:

```
if let p = a?.otherClass?.someProperty
{
    println (p)
}
else
{
    println ("no property available")
}
```

If any optional in the chain returns a nil value, the entire expression returns nil.

The use of optional chaining isn't restricted to reading property values; we can also write them like this:

```
a?.otherClass?.someProperty = 6
```

The statement will return nil if the assignment failed because some part of the optional chain returned nil, which can be tested like this:

```
if (a?.otherClass?.someProperty = 6) == nil
{
    // unable to write the property
}
```

You can call methods using optional chaining, as follows:

```
a?.otherClass?.someMethod()
```

Again, the method call will return nil if the call failed because some part of the chain returned nil. Even if the method normally returns a nonoptional value, it will always be returned as an optional when used in an optional chain context.

You can also use optional chaining with subscripts:

```
a?.otherClass?[1]
// returns nil, or "getter for [1] called"

a?.otherClass?[3] = "Optional chaining is neat"
// returns nil if the assignment fails
```

Program Flow

Swift includes the usual selection of loops and conditional execution features. Most of these are superficially the same as their counterparts in C-like languages, but in some cases (e.g., the switch statement) they offer considerably expanded and safer functionality.

Loops

Swift provides the standard loop constructs that you would expect in a programming language, including for, while, and do-while loop variants.

for-condition-increment loops

The for-condition-increment loop is functionally the same as the for loop in C. The loop consists of an initialization phase, a test, an increment, and a set of statements that are executed for each iteration of the loop. Here's an example:

```
for initialization; condition; increment
{
    statements
}
```

The three phases work as follows:

- The initialization phase sets up the conditions for the start of the loop (typically, initializing a loop counter).

- The condition tests whether the loop's termination condition has been met—whenever this evaluates to true, the statements in the body of the loop are executed once.

- The increment phase adjusts some variable or value that forms part of the condition test to ensure that a stopping condition can be reached (typically, incrementing the loop counter).

It is possible that the statements in the body of the loop will never execute. For this to happen, the condition would have to evaluate to false the first time it was executed.

The body of the loop defines a new scope, inside which local variables and constants can be defined. These go out of scope as soon as the loop terminates, and their values are lost.

The most familiar version of this loop would be as follows:

```
for var i=0; i<10; i++
{
    println ("\(i)")
}
```

Note the following:

- Semicolons must separate the three expressions that define the setup, test, and increment phases.

- Unlike C, parentheses are optional around the setup, test, and increment code.

for-in loops

You use the for-in loop to iterate over collections of things, such as the elements of an array or dictionary, the characters in a string, or a range of numbers.

Here's the general format:

```
for index in collection
{
    statements
}
```

In the following example, which iterates over a range of numbers, the loop index variable (i) takes on the value of the next number in the range each time through the loop:

```
for i in 3...8
{
    println (i)
}
```

The example that follows iterates over the contents of an array. The loop index variable (i) takes on the value of the next entry in the array each time through the loop (see also the section "Iterating Over Arrays" on page 45):

```
var microprocessors = ["Z80", "6502", "i386"]
for i in microprocessors
{
    println (i)
}
// prints:
// Z80
// 6502
// i386
```

This next example iterates over the contents of a dictionary. A tuple is used as the loop index, so that for each iteration, we get the next key and its associated value (see also the section "Iterating Over Dictionaries" on page 50):

```
var vehicles = ["bike":2, "trike":3, "car":4, "lorry":18]
for (vehicle, wheels) in vehicles
{
    println (vehicle)
}
```

```
// prints:
// car
// lorry
// trike
// bike
```

The preceding example also demonstrates that dictionaries are stored in arbitrary order.

while loops

As in C, while loops test a condition ahead of the loop body; only if the condition evaluates to true is the loop body executed. The general format is as follows:

```
while condition
{
    statements
}
```

You can use the while loop to replicate the functionality of the for-condition-increment loop, as follows:

```
var count = 0;
while (count < 10)
{
    println (count)
    count ++;
}
```

The condition is tested before the body of the loop is executed. If it evaluates to false the first time it is executed, the statements in the body of the loop will never execute.

do-while loops

do-while loops test the termination condition at the end of the loop, rather than at the start. This means that the statements in the body of the loop are guaranteed to be executed at least once. Loop execution continues until the condition evaluates to false.

The general format for a do-while loop looks like this:

```
do
{
    statements
} while condition
```

Here is an example:

```
var t = 0;
do
{
    println (t)
    t++;
} while (t < 10)
```

Early termination of loops

You can use a `continue` statement anywhere in the body of the loop to stop the current iteration and begin the next iteration.

To terminate the loop, you use a `break` statement anywhere in the body of the loop, which continues execution at the next statement after the loop.

Conditional Execution

There are two statements in Swift that support conditional execution of blocks of code: the `if-else` statement and the `switch` statement.

if-else

The `if` statement tests a condition, and executes a block of code only if that condition evaluates to `true`.

Here's the simple form:

```
if condition
{
    // statements to execute
}
```

Note that unlike C and many other languages, parentheses are optional around the condition.

Also unlike C, *the braces are required*, even if only a single statement is to be executed when the condition evaluates to `true`.

The if statement has an optional else clause. If the condition evaluates to false, the statement(s) in the else clause is executed:

```
if condition
{
    // statements to execute when condition met
}
else
{
    // statements to execute when condition not met
}
```

In all but one situation, braces are required around the statements in the else clause. That situation is when the else clause is immediately followed by another if, as demonstrated here:

```
if condition
{
    println ("shouldn't see this")
}
else if condition
{
    println ("should see this")
}
```

You can chain multiple if statements in this way, optionally ending with a final else clause.

switch

The switch statement provides an alternative (and more concise) way to express a series of condition tests, which you would otherwise implement by using a chain of if-else statements.

The basic structure of the statement is as follows:

```
switch expression
{
    case valueSequence1:
        // statements to execute
    case valueSequence2:
        // statements to execute
    case valueSequence3:
        // statements to execute
}
```

```
    default:
        // statements to execute
}
```

The *expression* is evaluated, and the result is compared to each of the values associated with each case clause. If a match is found, the statements that form part of the matching case are executed. If no match is found, the statements that follow the optional default clause are executed.

Each case may contain a single value or a series of values separated by commas, as shown here:

```
case 2, 4, 6:
```

The switch statement in Swift is considerably enhanced compared to its counterpart in C-like languages. Here are the notable differences:

- The case clauses must be exhaustive (all possible values of expression must match a case, or there must be a default case to catch those that aren't); otherwise, the compiler will report an error.

- Execution of statements attached to a case clause will not fall through into another case unless this behavior is explicitly enabled with the fallthrough keyword (this prevents a common error in C, where a break statement may have been accidentally omitted).

- Every case must contain at least one executable statement.

- If more than one case matches, the first matching case is the one that is used.

- A single case can test for a match against a range of values.

- You can use tuples to test multiple values in a single case.

- The case clause can use an optional where clause to further refine the case match (see the section "The where qualifier" on page 78).

- The break statement is not required to prevent fall-through into the next case, but you can use it as a "no-operation" statement to terminate a case and continue execution at the next statement after the switch statement. This is useful when you need to match a specific case and exclude it ahead of another more general case which would otherwise include it.

Here is a simple example of a switch statement with multiple cases:

```
var a = "c"
switch a
{
    case "a", "e", "i", "o", "u":
        println("this letter is a vowel")
    case "b", "d", "g", "k", "p", "t":
        println("this letter may be a plosive sound in "
                + "English")
        fallthrough
    case "c", "f", "h", "j", "l", "m", "n", "q", "r", "s",
        "v", "w", "x", "y", "z":
        println("this letter is a consonant")
    default:
        println("this letter doesn't interest me")
}
```

Let's analyze this example a little closer:

- If a match is found in the first case clause, a message is printed indicating the letter is a vowel, and execution continues at the next statement after the switch statement.

- If a match is found in the second case clause, the println() function is called, but the fallthrough keyword causes execution to continue into the statement(s) defined as part of the next case clause (in this example, a second println() function is called).

Matching ranges in a case clause. Here is an example of a switch statement that uses ranges in the case clause:

```
var marbles = 600
switch marbles
{
    case 0:
        println("you've lost your marbles!")
    case 1:
        println("I see you have a marble")
    case 2...5:
        println("I see you have some marbles")
    case 6...10:
        println("That's quite a handful of marbles!")
    case 10...99:
        println("That's lots and lots of marbles")
    default:
        println("Were marbles on sale?")
}
```

Using tuples in a case clause. This next example demonstrates a crude class scheduling case statement, in which students in different grades (7–10) and of different genders ("M," "F") are scheduled for specific activities on different days of the week:

```
let year = 9                   // 7-10
let gender: Character = "M"    // "M" or "F"
let weekday = "Fri"            // "Mon" through "Fri"

let record = (gender, year, weekday)

switch record
{
    case ("M", 7...8, "Mon"):
        println ("Sports: Cricket")
    case ("F", 7...8, "Mon"):
        println ("Sports: Netball")
    case ("M", 9...10, "Tue"):
        println ("Sports: Football")
    case ("F", 9...10, "Tue"):
        println ("Sports: Softball")
    case (_, 7...8, "Wed"):
        println ("Music")
    case (_, 9...10, "Wed"):
        println ("Theater")
    case (_, 7...10, "Thu"):
        println ("Sciences")
    case (_, 7...10, "Fri"):
        println ("Humanities")
```

```
        default:
            println("nothing scheduled or invalid input")
}
// outputs "Humanities"
```

In the preceding example, the underscore (_) is used in some cases to match all possible values. This example also demonstrates matching a range of values (e.g., all students in grades 7–10, regardless of gender, study Humanities on Fridays).

Value binding with tuples and ranges. Because a tuple in a switch case matches a range of inputs, you can use let or var *value binding* in a case clause to assign a temporary name to, or make a temporary copy of, part of a matched value, as shown here:

```
switch record
{
    // ... preceding cases
    case (_, let yr, "Thu"):
        println ("Sciences - customized for year \(yr)")
    // subsequent cases...
}
```

In this example, the second component of the tuple still matches any input value. We use the let keyword to make a temporary local constant named yr; thus, we can subsequently use whatever value that might be in the case statement. We could also have used the var keyword to create a mutable copy of the value and then modify that copy in the scope of the case clause.

The where qualifier. You use the where qualifier to further refine a case clause in a switch statement. In the following example, we use the where clause with a value bound to the day of the week to match cases in which students are of either gender, in year 7, and the day is any day that begins with the letter "T":

```
switch record
{
    // ... preceding cases
    case (_, 7, let day) where day.hasPrefix("T"):
        println ("Home Economics")
```

```
    // subsequent cases...
}
```

Statement labels

You can precede switch statements and loop constructs by an optional label, which you can then use as an argument to a break or continue statement to indicate to which switch or loop that break or continue should apply.

Statement labels precede the switch or loop construct as follows:

```
label: do
{
    // some loop content
} while (someCondition)
```

Or alternatively:

```
label: switch expression
{
    // cases
}
```

Here's a simple example of nested loops with a continue statement that causes early termination under some conditions:

```
outerloop: for var i=1; i<10; i++
{
    for var j=1; j<10; j++
    {
        if ((i == 6) && ((i * j) >= 30))
            { continue outerloop }
        println (i * j)
    }
    println ("-")
}
```

Without the use of the statement label, the continue statement would skip the inner println function in some circumstances, but it would always execute nine inner loops for each outer loop. The presence of the label changes this, because it causes early termination of the inner loop in some circumstances and affects the overall number of iterations of both loops.

Using switch with enumerations

You can use an *enumeration* as the value of a switch statement that is to be matched against each case clause, as illustrated here:

```
enum TravelClass
{
    case First, Business, Economy
}

var thisTicket = TravelClass.First

switch thisTicket
{
    case .First:
        println ("Cost is $800")
    case .Business:
        println ("Cost is $550")
    case .Economy:
        println ("Cost is $200")
}
// outputs "Cost is $800"
```

Because switch statements must be exhaustive, all possible enumeration values must be checked, or there must be a default clause. See the section "Enumerations" on page 112 for more information.

Classes

As in Objective-C, a Swift class is a flexible entity that encapsulates properties (or data) and the methods that operate on them. You can derive classes from other classes (a feature called *inheritance*), in which case the derived class is referred to as the *subclass*, and the class from which it is derived is referred to as the *superclass*.

Unlike Objective-C, in which all classes are subclasses of NSObject, Swift allows for classes that are not derived from other classes. Such a class is referred to as *base class*.

From an implementation perspective, another significant difference is that code imported from other modules or frameworks in Swift does not use a separate header file. There is no separation of declarations and definitions. With Swift, the definition serves as the declaration.

Defining a Base Class

You declare a base class by using the following syntax:

```
class ClassName
{
    // property, member and related definitions
}
```

Here is an example of a simple base class that could be used to store a description of a microprocessor:

```
class Processor
{
    var dataWidth = 0
    var addressWidth = 0
    var registers = 0
    var name = ""
}
```

When it's defined, a class is like a new type: you can create variables or constants whose type is the class name, or use instances of the class in dictionaries and arrays as you would for built-in types.

NOTE

By convention, class names begin with an uppercase letter and use camel case for the remainder of the class name. Property and method names begin with a lowercase letter and use camel-case for the remainder of the name.

Thus, if you were to use a class for storing information relating to employees, you might name it EmployeeRecord, but not employeeRecord or employee_record.

The four variables defined in the class in the previous example are called *properties*. In other languages, they are variously called *instance variables*, *ivars*, or *data members*.

You must initialize properties that can store values. In the example, they are initialized with an assignment (dataWidth = 0). Alternatively, you can initialize them by using a separate initialization method, which is described in the section "Initialization" on page 100 later in the book.

Instances

You can think of a class as a recipe for constructing something, but it isn't the something that is actually constructed. We call the entity made from the recipe an *instance* or an *object*. In the same way, Int is a type of data, and a variable of type Int is an instance of that type of data.

You create instances of simple classes, such as the Processor class shown in the example in the previous section, by using the class name followed by empty parentheses, as shown here:

```
let proc = Processor()
```

This process, referred to as *instantiation*, constructs a new instance of the Processor class and creates a variable called proc that refers to it.

After you've created an instance, you can access its properties and modify them by using *dot syntax*:

```
proc.name = "Z80"
proc.dataWidth = 8
println (proc.name)
```

NOTE

You might wonder why proc can be declared as an immutable constant (with let), and yet we can modify its properties. Although proc itself is immutable (and cannot later be used to refer to a different instance of the class), it is a *reference* to an instance of the class that *is* mutable. There is currently no way in Swift to create an immutable instance of a class that has mutable properties.

At this level, classes are not substantially different to structs in C. The usefulness of classes comes through methods that we can add to them which can use and manipulate the properties of the class.

Because classes are reference types, new copies are not made during assignment. Consider this code:

```
var newProc = proc
```

Upon execution, newProc is a reference to the same object as proc. We can verify this by modifying a property of proc and checking that same property of newProc:

```
proc.name = "6502"
println (newProc.name)
// will output "6502"
```

You can test that proc and newProc refer to the same instance by using Swift's *identicality* operators (=== and !==). These operators test whether two references are to the same object:

```
if (proc === newProc)
{
    println ("same")
}
// will output "same"
```

Properties

Properties are values that are associated with a class or an instance of a class and the methods for accessing them. When they are associated with each instance of a class, they are known as *instance properties*, and when they are associated with the class itself, they are known as *type properties*. Properties can be stored values or they can be computed from other properties or values at runtime.

Stored properties

Stored properties are those for which space in memory is allocated to store the property's value. This is in contrast to *computed properties* (discussed a little later) for which no such space is allocated.

You declare stored properties with var (if they are to be mutable) or let (if they are to be immutable) inside the class definition. In the Processor example from earlier, dataWidth, address

Width, registers, and name are all examples of stored properties.

You access stored properties by using dot syntax, as demonstrated here:

```
proc.name = "6502"
// assigns "6502" to the name property of the proc instance
println (proc.dataWidth)
// outputs the dataWidth property of the proc instance
```

NOTE

You can define stored properties for both classes and structures.

Computed properties

Like computed variables, computed properties do not store a value but are methods that look like properties. They are defined in terms of a *getter* (identified with the keyword get, which returns the computed property) and a *setter* (identified with the keyword set, which might initialize the conditions that affect the value returned by the getter). You can also use the getter and setter to read and write other properties. You define a computed property as follows:

```
class someClass
{
    var propertyName: someType
    {
        get
        {
            // code that computes and returns
            // a value of someType
        }
        set(valueName)
        {
            // code that sets up conditions using valueName
        }
    }
}
```

valueName is optional. It is used to refer to the value passed into the set method. If you omit it, you can refer to the parameter by using the default name of newValue.

The setter is optional. If the setter is not used, the get clause is not required, and all that is needed is code to compute and return a value:

```
class someClass
{
    var propertyName: someType
    {
        // compute and return a value of someType
    }
}
```

After a computed property is defined, it is used exactly like any other property. If its name is used in an expression, the getter is called. If it is assigned a value, the setter is called.

Here is an example of a simple class named Rect that represents a rectangle in terms of a corner point, a width and a height, and defines a computed property called area to return the area of the Rect:

```
class Rect
{
    var x = 0.0, y = 0.0
    var width = 0.0, height = 0.0
    var area: Double { return (width * height) }
}
```

You could use this as follows:

```
var q = Rect()
q.width = 2.7
q.height = 1.4
q.area
// returns 3.78
```

NOTE

You can define computed properties for classes, structures, and enumerations.

Property observers

Property observers are functions that you can attach to stored properties and that are called when the value of the property is about to change (identified with the willSet keyword) or after it has changed (identified with the didSet keyword). The declaration looks as follows:

```
class Observer
{
    var name: String = ""
    {
        willSet(valueName)
        {
            // code called before the value is changed
        }
        didSet(valueName)
        {
            // code called after the value is changed
        }
    }
}
```

Both *valueName* identifiers (and their enclosing parentheses) are optional.

The willSet function is called immediately before the property is about to be changed (except for assignment during initialization). The new value is visible inside willSet as either *value Name*, or newValue if *valueName* was not specified. The function can't prevent the assignment from happening and can't change the value that will be stored in the property.

The didSet function is called immediately after the property has been changed (except for assignment during initialization). The old value is visible inside didSet as either *valueName* or old Value if *valueName* was not specified.

When creating a subclass, you can override properties of the superclass and then add property observers to them, allowing you to create new behaviors which the designer of the superclass did not plan for or consider.

Instance versus type properties

For most applications of classes, properties are associated with each instance of the class. Using the Processor class example from earlier, each microprocessor has a different name, different numbers of registers, and potentially different widths for their data and address paths. Each instance of the class requires its own set of these property values. Properties used in this way are called *instance* properties.

Some applications only require a single instance of a property for the entire class. Consider a class that records employee data and must keep a record of the next available ID for a new employee. This ID should not be stored in each instance, but it does need to be associated with the class in some way.

For such purposes, Swift provides *type properties*, which are properties associated with the class, not with a specific instance of the class. The same feature is referred to generically as a *class variable*, or in C++, Java, and C#, as a *static member variable*.

Computed type properties

When you're declaring a computed type property for a class, precede the type property's definition with the keyword `class`. The syntax for creating a read/write computed type property is as follows:

```
class SomeClass
{
    class var someComputedProperty: SomeType
    {
        get { return SomeType }
        set(valueName)
        {
            // do something with valueName
            // that sets the property
        }
    }
}
```

valueName is optional. It is used to refer to the value passed into the set function. If you omit it, you can refer to the parameter by using the default name of `newValue`.

If you want a read-only computed type property, omit the set definition. In this case, you can also omit the `get` keyword and reduce the var body to just the code that calculates and returns the desired value.

Constant properties

You can declare properties as constants by using the keyword `let`. Unlike regular constants, constant properties do not need to be assigned a value when they are defined. Instead, the setting of their value can be deferred until the class is initialized.

The following example demonstrates a simple class that includes an uninitialized constant property, `cp`, the value of which is set by the initializer function:

```
class DemoClass
{
    let cp: Int

    init(v: Int)
```

```
    {
        self.cp = v
    }
}

var demoClass = DemoClass (v: 8)
demoClass.cp
// returns 8
```

When using constant properties, you should note the following:

- Constant properties can only be initialized by the class in which they are defined; they cannot be initialized in a subclass.

- A constant property's value can be modified during initialization, but it must have a value before the initialization process has completed.

Methods

Methods are functions that are either associated with a class (in which case, they are known as *type methods*) or with every instance of a class (in which case, they are known as *instance methods*).

You define methods like functions inside the class definition, as in the following example, which revises the earlier example of the Rect class to use a method to return the area of the rectangle:

```
class Rect
{
    var x = 0.0, y = 0.0
    var width = 0.0, height = 0.0
    func area() -> Double
    {
        return width * height
    }
}
```

The method is called using dot syntax, as in this example:

```
var q = Rect()
q.width = 5.0
q.height = 2.0
q.area()
// returns 10.0
```

Local and external parameter names

In a function definition, parameter names are local unless an
external parameter name is explicitly declared or the local
parameter name is preceded by a # character. In this next
example, sourceString and searchString are both internal
parameter names:

```
func search (sourceString: String, searchString: String)
    -> Int { … }
```

This is in contrast to method definitions where, by default, all
parameter names *except* the first are both local *and* external.
The first parameter name is local unless preceded by an external parameter name or preceded by a #.

This difference in the default behavior between functions and
methods encourages the writing of method definitions in Swift
that are called in a manner that closely matches the style of
Objective-C method calls.

Consider this example, which introduces a new string-related
class with search capability:

```
class SomeStringClass
{
    func searchFor(searchString: String,
        startingAt: Int) -> Int
    {
        // return result of search
    }
}
```

In the searchFor() method defined in this class, searchString
is a local parameter name, whereas startingAt is both a local
and an external parameter name. The function facilitates
searching an instance of the string class by using this syntax:

```
var haystack = SomeStringClass()
haystack.searchFor("needle", startingAt: 0);
```

Let's break this down further:

- If you want the first parameter to have an external parameter name, either precede the local name with the external name or precede the local name with # to use the local name as the external name.

- For the second and subsequent parameters, if you want to prevent the definition of an external name, precede the local name with _ (an underscore character).

- For the second and subsequent parameters, if you want to define your own external name, precede the local name with the desired external name.

Self

Every instance of a class (and other types) has an automatically generated property named self which refers to that instance. Consider an extended version of our Rect class:

```
class Rect
{
    var x = 0.0, y = 0.0
    var width = 0.0, height = 0.0
    func area() -> Double
    {
        return width * height
    }
    func sameSizeAs(width: Double, _ height:Double) -> Bool
    {
        return width == self.width && height == self.height
    }
}
```

In the area() method, both width and height are properties of the instance, and the return statement could have explicitly referred to them thus:

```
return self.width * self.height
```

But this is not necessary, because in method calls, self is normally implied whenever properties or methods of that class are used.

The exception is when a parameter name for a method is the same as a property name for the class, such as occurs with the sameSizeAs() method. Parameter names take precedence over property names in methods; therefore, self must be explicitly used to differentiate the width and height properties from the width and height parameters.

Defining type methods

When defining a type method for a class, you must precede the method's definition with the keywords class func, as in the following example:

```
class AClass
{
    class func aTypeMethod()
    {
        // implementation
    }
}
```

Despite appearances, this is not a nested class definition.

To call a type method for a class, precede it with the class name using dot syntax:

```
AClass.aTypeMethod()
```

To call the same method from within other methods defined for the class, you can omit the class name because it is equivalent to self.

A type method can access other type methods defined in the class as well as computed type properties defined in the class.

Subscripts

In Swift, you can define subscript methods for your own classes, which make it possible for you to use *subscript syntax* to read and write values appropriate for an instance of your class.

Subscript syntax is how you access members of arrays and dictionaries, as demonstrated here:

```
var m = [Int](count:10, repeatedValue:0)
m[1] = 45;
m[2] = m[1] * 2

var cpus = ["BBC Model B":"6502", "Lisa":"68000",
            "TRS-80":"Z80"]
let cpu = cpus["BBC Model B"]
```

Subscript syntax affords both reading and writing of values, and adheres to the following general pattern:

```
class SomeClass
{
    subscript(index: someIndexType) -> someReturnType
    {
        get
        {
            // return someReturnType based on index
        }
        set(valueName)
        {
            // write valueName based on index
        }
    }
}
```

You can omit the *valueName* parameter name, in which case the parameter to be written can be accessed as newValue.

Here's an example class that can represent byte values. It also defines a subscript method by which you can access individual bits as though the byte is an array of bits:

```
class Byte
{
    var d: UInt8 = 0

    subscript(whichBit: UInt8) -> UInt8
    {
        get { return (d >> whichBit) & 1 }
        set
```

```
        {
            let mask = 0xFF ^ (1 << whichBit)
            let bit = newValue << whichBit
            d = d & mask | bit
        }
    }
}
```

After it is defined, you can use the class like this:

```
var b = Byte()
b[0] = 1
// b is now 0000 0001, or 1
b[2] = 1
// b is now 0000 0101, or 5
b[0] = 0
// b is now 0000 0100, or 4
```

Here are some additional things you can do in relation to subscripts:

- For a read-only subscript, omit the set definition—in this case, you can also omit the get keyword and reduce the subscript body to just the code that calculates and returns the desired value.

- Subscript parameters aren't limited to single integer values; you can declare a subscript method that takes any number of floats, strings, or other types that suit your requirements.

- You can define multiple overloaded subscript methods as long as they take different numbers and/or types of parameters, or return different types of value. Swift will determine the appropriate method to call using type inferencing.

Member Protection

Swift provides a mechanism for controlling access to properties, methods, and subscripts of classes as part of a broader access control system. Read the section "Access Control" on page 119 for more information.

Inheritance: Deriving One Class from Another

You can define new classes in terms of existing classes. In doing so, the new class is said to *inherit* all of the properties and methods of the existing class; the new class is *derived* from the existing class.

A common example used to illustrate inheritance is that of 2D geometric shapes. The generic *base class* contains methods and properties that should be common to all shapes, such as color, fill, line thickness, and perhaps origin or enclosing rectangle. Derived classes include actual geometric shapes, such as lines, circles, ellipses, quads, polygons, and so on. Each of these introduce new methods and properties that are specific to that shape (such as a draw method and properties to store the geometric details), but all inherit from the base class the common set of properties and methods that all shapes have.

In Swift, you derive one class from another by using this syntax:

```
class NewClassName: BaseClassName
{
    // property and method definitions for the new class
}
```

Overriding Superclass Entities

When one class is derived from another, the new class is called the *subclass*, and the class from which it is derived is called the *superclass*. Although much of the time a subclass will add its own properties and methods to those inherited from the superclass, a subclass also has the ability to *override* methods and properties of the superclass by redefining them itself.

To override something already defined in a superclass, you must precede its definition in the subclass with the `override` keyword. This is a signal to the Swift compiler that the redefinition is intentional, and that you haven't accidentally created a method or property with the same name.

In Swift, you can override methods, properties, and subscripts.

Accessing overridden superclass entities

A derived class can use the super prefix in overriding definitions to access the superclass version of that entity. Following
are the ways in which you can do this:

- To access an overridden method, call it with
  super.*methodName*().

- To access an overridden property, refer to it as
  super.*propertyName* in the getter, setter, or observer
  definitions.

- To access an overridden subscript, use super[*index
  Value*].

Overriding properties

You can't actually override a property in a superclass with your
own property (it wouldn't make sense to duplicate the storage
space), but you can override a property in order to provide
your own custom getter and setter for the superclass instance,
or add a property observer so that you can be informed when
the property value changes.

Earlier in this section, we introduced the Rect class for storing
arbitrary rectangles. The example that follows creates a derived
class, Square(), that overrides the width and height properties
with new getters and setters which ensure that the height and
width always match, and therefore that instances of the Square
class are always in fact square:

```
class Square: Rect
{
    override var width: Double
    {
        get { return super.width }
        set
        {
            super.width = newValue
            super.height = newValue
        }
```

```
    }
    override var height: Double
    {
        get { return super.height }
        set
        {
            super.width = newValue
            super.height = newValue
        }
    }
}
```

Note that the getter and setter still access the properties that are stored in the superclass via the super prefix. Here is an example of the class in use:

```
var s = Square()
s.width = 20.0
s.height = 10.0
s.area()
// returns 100.0
s.width
// returns 10.0 (not 20.0)
```

When overriding properties, note the following:

- You can override inherited read-only properties as read/write properties, by defining both a getter and setter.

- You *cannot* override inherited read/write properties as read-only properties.

- If you provide a setter, you must also provide a getter (even if it only returns the superclass property unmodified).

- You can override inherited mutable properties (declared with var) with property observers, but you cannot override inherited immutable properties (declared with let) in this way (because property observers are intended to observe *writes* to the property).

- You cannot override a property with both a setter and an observer (because the setter can act as the observer).

Overriding methods and subscripts

To override a method or a subscript that exists in the superclass, precede the method or subscript name in the derived class with the override keyword.

In the earlier subscript discussion, we introduced a Byte class that included a subscript method which made it possible for us to access each bit of a byte as though it were an array of bits, using subscript syntax.

One serious problem with this class is that it does not perform bounds-checking on either the subscript value or the value to be written. If we refer to a bit position higher than 7, the program will terminate because the mask assignment in the setter will generate an overflow. If we assign a bit value of something other than 0 or 1, the assignment will happen, but it will pollute other bits in the byte property that we're presenting as the array of bits.

For the purpose of illustration, let's create a safe derived class that overrides the subscript definition to ensure that these values can't exceed their appropriate values:

```
class SafeByte: Byte
{
    override subscript(whichBit: UInt8) -> UInt8
    {
        get { return super[whichBit & 0x07] }
        set { super[whichBit & 0x07] = newValue & 1 }
    }
}
```

Observe that this still uses the superclass implementation of the subscript function; it just sanitizes the bit value and bit position before doing so.

Preventing Overrides and Subclassing

Prepending the keyword final to a property, method, or subscript definition prevents that entity from being overridden in a derived class. Here is a modified version of our Rect class that uses the final keyword to prevent the width and height properties from being overridden:

```
class Rect
{
    var x = 0.0, y = 0.0
    final var width = 0.0, height = 0.0
    // rest of definition
}
```

Note that the use of final in this context does not mean that the values of width and height are locked; it just means that the properties cannot be overridden in a subclass.

This change means that our Square class from earlier would no longer compile, because it overrides these properties with a custom setter and getter.

You can also use the final keyword in front of a class definition to prevent that class from being subclassed.

Initialization

Initialization is the process of setting up appropriate default values for stored properties in a new instance of a class, structure, or enumeration. The process is similar to a constructor in C++, C#, or Java, or the Init selector in Objective-C. It ensures that a new instance is ready for use and does not contain random or uninitialized data.

Initialization happens automatically for a new instance of a class; you do not call the initializer explicitly, although you do need to call initializers in a superclass from the initializer of a derived class (see the section "Initialization and Inheritance" on page 106 for more information).

You can initialize stored properties by either assignment of default values in the class definition or by defining one or more init() functions in the class. The Byte class we introduced earlier demonstrates initialization by assignment:

```
class Byte
{
    var d: UInt8 = 0
    // rest of class definition
}
```

For more complex classes, it is common to write one or more init() functions to manage the process of instantiating a new instance of an object. For classes, Swift supports two kinds of initialization function: *designated initializers* and *convenience initializers.*

A designated initializer must initialize all of the properties of a class. In a subclass, it must initialize all of the properties defined in that subclass and then call a designated initializer in the superclass to continue the initialization process for any inherited properties.

A convenience initializer provides a way to call a designated initializer with some of the designated initializer's parameters set to common default values.

A designated initializer is defined by using the following syntax:

```
class ClassName
{
    init(parameterList)
    {
        // statements to initialize instance
    }
    // rest of class definition
}
```

A convenience initializer is defined by using the following syntax:

```
class ClassName
{
    convenience init(parameterList)
    {
        // statements to initialize instance
    }
    // rest of class definition
}
```

Here as some important characteristics of the initialization process:

- If a property has a property observer, that observer is not called when the property is initialized.

- Properties whose type is *optional* are automatically initialized to nil if you do not separately initialize them.

- Immutable properties (declared with let) can be modified during initialization, even if assigned a default value in the class definition.

- A designated initializer is the main initializer for a class. Most classes will only have one, but more than one is allowed: for example, one with no arguments that sets all properties to default values, and one with arguments that serve as initialization values for specific properties.

- A designated initializer *must* call a designated initializer for its superclass.

- Convenience initializers are optional secondary initializers; they *must* call another initializer in the same class.

- A convenience initializer's execution *must* eventually lead to the execution of a designated initializer.

Swift also supports *deinitializers*, which are invoked automatically immediately before an object is deallocated (see the section "Deinitialization" on page 107 for more information).

Designated initializers

Our Rect class demonstrated initialization by assignment in the class definition:

```
class Rect
{
    var x = 0.0, y = 0.0
    var width = 0.0, height = 0.0
    // rest of definition
}
```

We could rewrite this to use a designated initializer function instead, like this:

```
class Rect
{
    var x, y, width, height: Double
    init()
    {
        x = 0.0; y = 0.0
        width = 0.0; height = 0.0
    }
    // remainder of class definition
}
```

This default init(), without parameters, is the initializer that is called when you create a new object with no initialization parameters, as in the following:

```
var q = Rect()
```

You can create additional initializers, each of which take different numbers and/or types of parameters. The following extended version of the Rect class includes two different designated initializer methods, either of which will be called depending on how the Rect is instantiated:

```
class Rect
{
    var x, y, width, height: Double
    init()
    {
        x = 0.0; y = 0.0
        width = 0.0; height = 0.0
    }
    init(x: Double, y: Double,
        width: Double, height: Double)
    {
        self.x = x
        self.y = y
        self.width = width
        self.height = height
    }
}
```

Now, either init() method can be used to construct Rect instances:

```
var q = Rect()
var r = Rect(x: 2.0, y: 2.0, width: 5.0, height: 5.0)
```

Note that the second init() function has only defined internal parameter names, but the instantiation of r shows that they are externally visible.

NOTE

For init() functions, Swift will always generate an external parameter name if one hasn't been defined. Moreover, external parameter names (whether explicitly defined, or implicitly generated) *must* be used when the class is instantiated.

If you want to prevent the generation of an external parameter name, precede the internal parameter name with an underscore, like this:

```
class Rect
{
    var x, y, width, height: Double
    init()
    {
        x = 0.0; y = 0.0
        width = 0.0; height = 0.0
    }
    init(_ x: Double, _ y: Double,
        _ width: Double, _ height: Double)
    {
        self.x = x
        self.y = y
        self.width = width
        self.height = height
    }
}
```

Because there are now no external parameter names, new instances of the class can be created just by specifying the parameter values, as shown here:

```
var q = Rect(2.0, 2.0, 5.0, 5.0)
```

Convenience initializers

Convenience initializers are secondary initialization functions that must call some other initializer within the same class, and ultimately they must cause the execution of a designated initializer.

In the section "Defining a Base Class" on page 81, we introduced a simple class called Processor to represent microprocessors. Our use of this class might require frequent instantiation of a particular type of processor class, and hence support the inclusion of a convenience initializer:

```
class Processor
{
    var dataWidth = 0
    var addressWidth = 0
    var registers = 0
    var name = ""

    init (name: String, dWidth: Int, aWidth: Int, regs: Int)
    {
        self.name = name
        dataWidth = dWidth
        addressWidth = aWidth
        registers = regs
    }

    convenience init (eightbitName: String, regs: Int)
    {
        self.init(name: eightbitName, dWidth:8,
                    aWidth:16, regs: regs)
    }
}
```

Note that the convenience initializer defaults two of the four parameters required by the designated initializer, which it calls as self.init().

The convenience initializer is called when we construct a new instance, like this:

```
var p = Processor(eightbitName:"6502", regs:3)
```

Initialization and Inheritance

Hierarchies of classes introduce additional complexity into the way that initializers are defined and used, including the following:

- A designated initializer must set values for all properties introduced in its own class before calling a superclass initializer.

- A designated initializer must call a superclass initializer before setting the value of any inherited property.

- A convenience initializer must call another initializer in its class (convenience or designated) before setting the value of any property.

- Initializers cannot call instance methods, read instance properties, or refer to self until all properties introduced by the class and all properties of its superclass hierarchy have been initialized.

A derived class in Swift does not usually inherit initializers from a superclass, but there are two circumstances in which it does:

- If the derived class does not define any designated initializers of its own, it will automatically inherit all of the designated initializers of its superclass.

- If the derived class implements all of its superclass designated initializers, by any combination of defining them itself and inheriting them, it will automatically inherit all of its superclass convenience initializers.

Overriding initializers

You can override initialization functions in a derived class, but you must consider the following:

- To override a designated initializer, you *must* precede its definition with the keyword override.

- To override a convenience initializer, it must use the same number of parameters, with the same names and types, as the superclass initializer it is overriding, but you must *not* use the override keyword.

Required initializers

The required keyword, when used in front of an initializer, means that the initializer must be implemented in a derived class. Here are two issues to keep in mind:

- A required designated initializer *must* be redefined in the derived class.

- A required convenience initializer does not need to be redefined in the derived class if it will be automatically inherited, unless the inherited behavior is not desirable.

Deinitialization

Deinitialization is the process of cleaning up anything related to an instance of a class immediately before that instance is deallocated. The process is similar to a destructor in C++ and C#, or a finalize method in Java.

A deinitializer is declared by using the deinit keyword, as shown here:

```
class SomeClass
{
    // other parts of class definition
    deinit
    {
        // code to tidy up before deallocation
    }
}
```

The `deinit` function is called automatically and cannot be called directly.

A derived class inherits its superclass deinitializer, and the superclass deinitializer is automatically called at the end of the derived deinitializer's implementation.

Structures

In Swift, structures are closely related to classes (see "Classes" on page 80), which can be surprising for C and Objective-C programmers, but less surprising for those familiar with C++, in which classes and structs are also closely related.

Here are some notable similarities and differences:

- Like classes, structures can have properties, instance and type methods, subscripts, and initializers, and they can support extensions and protocols (see the sections "Extensions" on page 123 and "Protocols" on page 131).

- Structures can't inherit from or be derived from other structures and can't have deinitializers.

- Structures are *value types*, whereas classes are *reference types*. This means that structures are always copied when assigned or used as arguments to functions; they don't use reference counts.

The syntax for declaring a new structure is as follows:

```
struct StructureName
{
    // property, member and related definitions
}
```

Properties in Structures

Properties and property features in structures are largely iden-
tical to those of classes, and you should read the subsection
"Properties" on page 84 in "Classes" on page 80 to learn the
basics.

Like classes, structures support stored and computed properties, property observers, and constant properties.

Structures also support type (also known as class) properties.
Whereas classes introduce these by using the keyword class, in
structures they are introduced with the keyword static.

Methods in Structures

Structures can have instance methods, defined by using the
same syntax as they are with classes. The following example
demonstrates a structure for representing rectangles in terms of
a corner point, a width, and a height, and includes a method
area() that computes the area of the shape:

```
struct Rect
{
    var x = 0.0, y = 0.0, width = 0.0, height = 0.0

    func area() -> Double
    {
        return (width * height)
    }
}
```

Mutating Methods

By default, instance methods defined in a structure are not able to modify that entity's properties. You can enable this behavior, however, by defining the instance method as a *mutating method*.

The following example modifies our earlier Rect structure to include a mutating method embiggenBy(), which modifies the width and height properties:

```
struct Rect
{
    var x = 0.0, y = 0.0, width = 0.0, height = 0.0

    mutating func embiggenBy(size: Double)
    {
        width += size
        height += size
    }
}
```

A mutating method can also replace the current instance of the structure with a new instance by direct assignment to self.

Type Methods for Structures

When declaring a type method for a structure, precede the method's definition with the keyword static (in contrast to classes, for which the keyword class is used), as illustrated in this example:

```
struct AStruct
{
    static func aTypeMethod()
    {
        // implementation
    }
}
```

Type methods defined in structures can access other type methods and type properties defined for the same structure (indicated with the keyword static).

To call the type method for a structure, you precede it with the structure name using dot syntax, as shown here:

```
AStruct.aTypeMethod()
```

To call the same method from within other methods defined for the structure, the structure name can be omitted because it is equivalent to self.

Initializers in Structures

As with classes, there are a number of different ways that you can initialize a structure before it is used. The most obvious way is by assigning default values to stored property members during assignment, as in this example:

```
struct Rect
{
    var x=0.0, y=0.0, width=0.0, height=0.0
}
```

New instances of this structure can be instantiated without specifying any parameters:

```
var qq = Rect()
```

If no initializer methods are included in a structure definition, Swift will automatically create a *memberwise initializer* that allows each stored property to be specified during instantiation, such as the following:

```
var q = Rect(x:2.0, y:2.0, width:2.0, height:5.0)
```

If you require more flexibility than what is provided by either the memberwise initializer or default values, you can write your own init() method (or methods) to do custom initialization.

Initializer delegation in structures

For structures that include more than a few init() methods, you can use *initializer delegation*, by which one init() method calls another to carry out some part of the initialization process. Here is an example of a structure for implementing a Rect class that includes two different init() methods:

```
struct Rect
{
    var x, y, width, height: Double

    init(_ x: Double, _ y: Double,
        _ width: Double, _ height: Double)
    {
        self.x = x
        self.y = y
        self.width = width
        self.height = height
    }

    init()
    {
        self.init(0.0, 0.0, 0.0, 0.0)
    }

}
```

The first init() method provides a way to initialize the structure such that each initial property value is specified when the structure is instantiated:

```
var q = Rect(0.0, 0.0, 3.0, 4.0)
```

The second init() method provides another way to instantiate the structure, as in the following:

```
var r = Rect()
```

In this case, the second init() function delegates all of its work to the first init() function by using the self prefix, with each parameter set to 0. Only initializers are allowed to call other initializers in this way.

Enumerations

An enumeration is a user-defined type that consists of a set of named values. With enumerations, algorithms can be more naturally expressed by using the language of the problem set rather than having to manually map values from another type (such as Int) to some representation of the problem set.

For example, you might want to store information about the class of travel for a ticket. Without enumerations, you might use "1" to represent first class, "2" to represent business class, and "3" to represent economy class.

Using an enumeration, you could instead represent the classes as named values such as first, business, and economy.

Enumerations in Swift are considerably enhanced compared to their counterparts in C-based languages, and they share many characteristics with classes and structures. Following are some of the notable similarities and differences:

- Enumerations can have computed properties (but not stored properties), instance and type methods, and initializers (see also the section "Classes" on page 80).

- Enumerations support extensions and protocols (see the sections ""Extensions" on page 123" and "Protocols" on page 131).

- Enumerations can't inherit or be derived from other enumerations and can't have deinitializers.

The syntax for declaring a new enumeration is as follows:

```
enum EnumName
{
    // list(s) of enumeration member values
}
```

NOTE

By convention, enumeration names begin with an uppercase letter, and use camel case for the remainder of the enumeration name.

Using our travel class analogy, the example becomes thus:

```
enum TravelClass
{
    case First
    case Business
    case Economy
}
```

We can write the same definition more concisely, as demonstrated here:

```
enum TravelClass
{
    case First, Business, Economy
}
```

Unlike C, enumerations in Swift are not assigned equivalent integer values, but such values can be optionally assigned to them (see the section "Raw Member Values" on page 114).

Once defined, enumerations are used much like any other type:

```
var thisTicket = TravelClass.First
var thatTicket: TravelClass
thatTicket = .Economy
```

Note that dot syntax is required when referring to a named value from an enumeration. In the second assignment in the preceding example, the enumeration name is omitted because it can be inferred from the variable type, but the dot is still required.

Raw Member Values

In C, each member of an enumeration has an underlying integer value, and you can use that value in place of the member name. Swift does not assign values to enumeration members by default, but you can include values in the definition. These are called *raw values*. Moreover, raw values aren't limited to integer values; they can be strings, characters, or floating-point values, but all raw values for a given enumeration must be of the same type.

This example declares an enumeration with raw values of Int type:

```
enum AtomicNumber: Int
{
    case Hydrogen = 1
    case Helium = 2
    case Lithium = 3
    case Beryllium = 4
}
```

For enumerations where the raw value is of Int type, successive members will be given auto-incrementing raw values if no value is provided:

```
enum AtomicNumber: Int
{
    case Hydrogen = 1, Helium, Lithium, Beryllium
}
// Helium = 2, Lithium = 3, Beryllium = 4
```

The rawValue property in this example gives you access to a member's raw value:

```
AtomicNumber.Lithium.rawValue
// returns 3

var mysteryElement = AtomicNumber.Helium
mysteryElement.rawValue
// returns 2
```

The (rawValue: n) initializer lets you translates a raw value back its enumeration value, if one exists. Because there might be no member with the specified raw value, this returns an optional value, which must be unwrapped:

```
if let r = AtomicNumber(rawValue: 2)
{
    // r will have the value Helium
}
else
{
    // there was no matching member for the raw value 2
}
```

Associated Values

Raw member values are invariant (i.e., they are constant values that are associated with each enumeration member). Enumerations in Swift support another kind of value called an *associated value*. These are more like properties of a class—you can set each one differently for each instance of the enumeration.

You define associated values for an enumeration as follows:

```
enum EnumName
{
    case MemberName(SomeType [, SomeType...])
    case AnotherMemberName(SomeType [, SomeType...])
}
```

The associated value(s)—expressed as a tuple—can have one or more values, each of which can be of a different type.

Let's consider a concrete example. The term "network address" can be generically used to mean an address for the type of protocol being considered, even though network addresses for two different protocols might look very different from each other.

For example, an Ethernet MAC address consists of six 2-digit hex values separated by colons (e.g., "00:01:23:45:CD:EF"), whereas an IPv4 consists of four 8-bit unsigned values (or octets). We can represent this as an enumeration with associated values like this:

```
enum NetworkAddress
{
    case MAC(String)
    case IPv4(UInt8, UInt8, UInt8, UInt8)
}
```

When we define a variable of this enumeration type, we can associate IP addresses with each IPv4 case, and MAC addresses with each MAC case:

```
var routerAddress = NetworkAddress.IPv4(192, 168, 0, 1)
var dnsServerAddress = NetworkAddress.IPv4(8, 8, 8, 8)
var ethernetIF = NetworkAddress.MAC("00:DE:AD:BE:EF:00")
```

Note that the associated value is stored with the variable; it is not part of the enumeration. You can even reassign a different type of network address to an existing variable of that type and store a different type of associated value:

```
var someAddress = NetworkAddress.IPv4(192, 168, 0, 1)
someAddress = NetworkAddress.MAC("00:DE:AD:BE:EF:00")
someAddress = NetworkAddress.IPv4(10, 10, 0, 1)
```

To check for different types of network addresses, use a switch statement:

```
someAddress = NetworkAddress.IPv4(10, 10, 0, 1)
switch someAddress
{
    case .MAC:
        println ("got a MAC address")
    case .IPv4:
        println ("got an IP address")
}
// prints "got an IP address"
```

To access the associated value, use a switch statement with let value binding:

```
someAddress = NetworkAddress.MAC("00:DE:AD:BE:EF:00")
switch someAddress
{
    case let .MAC(theaddress):
        println ("got a MAC address of \(theaddress)")
    case let .IPv4(a, b, c, d):
        println ("got an IP address with" +
            "a low octet of \(d)")
}
// prints "got a MAC address of 00:DE:AD:BE:EF:00"
```

Methods in Enumerations

Enumerations can have instance methods, which you define using the same syntax as when defining classes. The following example extends our NetworkAddress enumeration to include a method getPrintable() that returns the associated value of either enumeration type as a string:

```
enum NetworkAddress
{
    case MAC(String)
    case IPv4(UInt8, UInt8, UInt8, UInt8)

    func getPrintable() -> String
    {
        switch self
        {
            case let .MAC(theAddress):
                return theAddress
            case let .IPv4(a, b, c, d):
                return ("\(a).\(b).\(c).\(d)")
        }
    }
}
```

You use this as follows:

```
var someAddress = NetworkAddress.IPv4(192, 168, 0, 1)
someAddress.getPrintable()
// returns "192.168.0.1"
someAddress = NetworkAddress.MAC("00:DE:AD:BE:EF:00")
someAddress.getPrintable()
// returns "00:DE:AD:BE:EF:00"
```

By default, instance methods defined in an enumeration are not able to modify the instance's value, but you can enable this behavior by defining the instance method as a *mutating method* (see the subsection "Mutating Methods" on page 110 in "Structures" on page 108).

Type Methods for Enumerations

To declare a type method for an enumeration, you precede the method's definition with the keyword static (in contrast to classes, where the keyword class is used), as shown in the following example:

```
enum AnEnumeration
{
    static func aTypeMethod()
    {
        // implementation
    }
}
```

Type methods defined in enumerations can access other type methods and type properties defined for the same enumerations (indicated with the keyword `static`).

To call a type method for an enumeration, precede it with the enumeration name using dot syntax, like so:

```
AnEnumeration.aTypeMethod()
```

To call the same method from within other methods defined for the same enumeration, you can omit the enumeration name because it is equivalent to `self`.

Access Control

Many object-oriented languages feature a method of access control for limiting access to members of classes. For example, C++ supports *public, protected,* and *private* access levels for data and function members of a class or structure.

Swift provides a similar mechanism, but it extends it to provide access control for higher-order types (classes, structures, and enumerations) as well as their members, and for globally defined values, such as functions and variables, type aliases, protocols, extensions, and generics.

The access control levels provided by Swift are *public, internal,* and *private.* Following are descriptions of each and some limitations on their use:

- Public entities are accessible from any source file in the module in which they are defined as well as any source file that imports that module.

- Internal entities are accessible from any source file in the module in which they are defined, but not from elsewhere. Internal access is the default access level that is applied in most cases for which access control is not otherwise specified.

- Private entities are only accessible within the source file in which they are defined (and thus are not even accessible from other source files that are part of the same module).

- It is not possible to specify an access level for an entity that is more open than the access level of its type. For example, if the class *SomeClass* has an access level of internal, it is not possible to define an instance of this class and assign it an access level of public.

- It is not possible to specify an access level for a member of an entity that is more open than the entity itself. For example, if the class *SomeClass* has an access level of internal, it is not possible for a member of the class to have an access level of public.

Specifying Access Control Levels

You specify access control levels by preceding the entity to which they refer with one of the keywords, public, internal, or private, as in the following:

```
public let APIVersion = "1.0.0"
private struct HashingRecord { }
internal class Byte { }
```

The access level specified for a type affects the default access level for its members:

- If a type's access is marked as private, its members will default to private.

- If a type's access is marked as public or internal, its members will default to internal—you need to explicitly declare members as public if you want them visible outside the current module, even if the containing entity itself is marked as public.

- If a type's access is not specified, it, and its members, will default to internal.

Earlier in the section on classes we introduced a Byte class that included a subscript definition that allowed us to treat a Byte object as an array of bits. If we were including this class in a framework for other programs to use, we would make the class and its subscript member public, but might want to make the variable that contains the stored value private, so that the implementation is opaque to callers:

```
public class UInt8
{
    private var d: UInt8 = 0

    public subscript(whichBit: UInt8) -> UInt8
    {
        // rest of subscript definition
    }
}
```

Other code that imported this library module would be able to create instances of the Byte class, and could set and get their value by subscript, but could not access the d property directly.

Default Access Control Levels

Although the default access level for most entities is internal, there are some exceptions and caveats that you might need to consider, which are presented in Table 6.

Table 6. Access control restrictions

Type	Default/available access level(s)
Constants, variables, properties	Constants, variables, and properties must have either the same access level as their type, or a more restrictive level. For example, a variable of type *SomeClass* that is marked internal cannot itself be marked as public.
Enumeration cases	The access level of the cases of an enumeration is the same as the access level of the enumeration itself (enumeration cases are not members in the usual sense).
Enumeration values	The default access level is the same as the access level of the enumeration with which the values are associated and cannot be overridden with a more restrictive access level.

Type	Default/available access level(s)
Extensions	When extending a class, structure, or enumeration, new members defined in the extension have the same default access level as members of the original entity:

- You can override the default for new members by specifying a different access level on the extension.

- The access level for new members can override the default but cannot be more open than the access level of the original entity.

- You cannot specify an access level on an extension that adds protocol conformance.

Type	Default/available access level(s)
Function	The default access level is the most restrictive of all of the function's parameter and return types. You can override the default but only with a more restrictive level.
Generics	The effective access level for generics is the most restrictive of the access level of the generic itself as well as the access level of any of its constraining types.
Getters, setters	The default access level for getters and setters is the same as the access level for the entity on which they are defined. The setter can have a more restrictive level than the getter (limiting modification of the entity without affecting its readability), which is specified by preceding the variable or property name with either `private(set)` or `internal(set)`.
Initializers	The default access level for initializers is the same as the access level of the class to which they belong. You can override the default for a custom initializer with a more restrictive level.

Type	Default/available access level(s)
Nested types	• Types defined within private types will also be private. • Types defined within internal types will default to the internal access level but can be made private. • Types defined within public types will default to the internal access level, and you can override with any access level.
Protocols	The default access level is internal, but you can override this with any level. Each requirement within the protocol has the same access level as the protocol itself, and this cannot be overridden.
Subclasses	The default access level is the same as that of the superclass, but you can override this with a more restrictive level. A subclass can override the implementation of an inherited class member and override that member's access level so long as it is not more open than the access level of the subclass.
Subscripts	The default access level for a subscript is the most restrictive of its index and return types. You can override this only with a more restrictive level.
Tuple	The only available access level is the most restrictive level of all of the types that comprise the tuple. You cannot override this because tuples are not explicitly defined like other types.
Type aliases	The default access level for a type alias is the same as that of the type that it aliases. You can override the default with a more restrictive level.

Extensions

Swift's extensions mechanism makes it possible for you to add new functionality to existing classes, structures, and enumerations, even if you did not create them yourself, and you do not have their source code. This is a hugely powerful feature and one which opens opportunities for extending Swift itself—if the language is missing a feature that you need, you can often add it yourself as an extension.

The basic syntax of an extension is as follows:

```
extension Type
{
    // code that extends Type
}
```

Extensions can only add new functionality to existing types; they cannot override existing properties, methods, subscripts, or any other functionality already defined in a type.

Computed Property Extensions

You can use extensions to add computed type properties and computed instance properties to an existing type, but you cannot use them to add stored properties or property observers.

Here is a simple extension that adds a computed property to the UInt class that returns a hex representation of the unsigned integer as a string:

```
extension UInt
{
    var asHex: String
    {
        var temp = self
        var result = ""
        let digits = Array("0123456789abcdef")
        while (temp > 0)
        {
            result = String(digits[Int(temp &
                        0x0f)]) + result
            temp >>= 4
        }
        return result
    }
}
```

With this extension in place, we can query the asHex property of any UInt type to get its hex equivalent as a string:

```
45.asHex
// returns "2d"
var s = 100.asHex
// stores "64" in a new String variable s
```

Initializer Extensions

You can use an extension to add convenience initializers to a class, but you cannot add delegated initializers or deinitializers.

You can also use an extension to add initializers to structures. If the structure does not define its own initializers, your extension initializer can call the default member-wise initializer if required to set all default property values.

Method Extensions

You can use extensions to add instance methods and type methods to an existing type. This example extends the Int type to provide a facility for converting an integer to a fixed-width string with leading spaces:

```
extension Int
{
    func asRightAlignedString(width: Int) -> String
    {
        var s = "\(self)"
        while (countElements(s) <= width)
        {
            s = " " + s
        }
        return s
    }
}

let x = -45
x.asRightAlignedString(5)
// returns "   -45"
```

An instance method added with an extension can modify the instance with the mutating keyword. This example extends the Double type with a method that truncates a double to its nearest integer value that is not larger than the original value:

```
extension Double
{
    mutating func trunc()
    {
        self = Double(Int(self))
    }
}

var d = 45.5
d.trunc()
// d is now 45.0
```

Subscript Extensions

Here is an example that extends the String class to support subscripted character referencing:

```
extension String
{
    subscript (i: Int) -> String
    {
        return String(Array(self)[i])
    }
}
```

To use this, follow a string with a subscript:

```
"Hello"[4]
// returns "o"
var a = "Alphabetical"
a[0]
// returns "A"
```

Earlier, in the introduction to classes, we presented a Byte class that included a subscript definition with which we could treat a Byte object as an array of bits. Using extensions, we can apply the same feature to the UInt8 type, as demonstrated here:

```
extension UInt8
{
    subscript(whichBit: UInt8) -> UInt8
    {
        get { return (self >> whichBit) & 1 }
        set
        {
            let mask = 0xFF ^ (1 << whichBit)
            let bit = (newValue & 1) << whichBit
```

```
            self = self & mask | bit
        }
    }
}

var b: UInt8 = 0
b[0] = 1
b[7] = 1
b
// returns 129
```

Checking and Casting Types

Swift is a strongly typed language, but there are times when some relaxation of type rules is warranted, and there are times when you want to check what an object's type is or downcast a reference to a subclass type.

Using Swift's is, as, and as? type casting operators, you can test types and protocol conformance, and downcast types and protocols.

Any and AnyObject

One Swift mechanism that provides type flexibility comes via the keywords AnyObject and Any, which are special built-in type aliases. AnyObject can represent an instance of any class, whereas Any can represent an instance of any type except for function types.

You can use these two type aliases to create complex entities. For example, an array that can store any type of data:

```
var a = [Any]()
a.append(2)
a.append(3.4)
a.append("crunch")
```

Or you can create a function that can take an instance of any class type:

```
func someFunc(t: AnyObject)
{
    // do something with t
}
```

Another example of where AnyObject is required is when call-ing Objective-C APIs that return an NSArray. Because an Objective-C array can contain arbitrary object types, it must be represented in Swift as an array of type [AnyObject]. To work with such an array, you will likely need to use Swift's type-casting operators to cast references to the array entries to an appropriate Swift class, such as a String.

Checking Types

You use the is operator to check whether an instance is of a specific type. Consider the following example of three classes A, B, and C. Note that B is a subclass of A:

```
class A { }
class B: A { }
class C { }

var a = A()
var b = B()
var c = C()
```

Next, we create a function that takes an instance of any object as a parameter and uses the is operator to check whether it is an instance of A:

```
func typeCheck(t: AnyObject) -> Bool
{
    return t is A
}

typeCheck(a) // true
typeCheck(b) // true
typeCheck(c) // false
```

The first typeCheck call returns true because a is an instance of class A. The second call also returns true, because b is an instance of B, which in turn is a subclass of A. The third call returns false because c is not of type A or a subclass of A.

Downcasting Types

Using downcasting, we can treat an instance of a class as an instance of one of its subclasses.

Consider the scaffolding in the example that follows for a system for representing geometric shapes. We start with a generic base class called shape and then define specific shapes as subclasses of the base class to represent circles and squares. Note that the subclasses have different functionality to one another. In this contrived example, one has a describe method, while the other has an identify method—a small difference purely for the sake of demonstration:

```
class Shape { }
class Square: Shape
{
    func describe()
    {
        println("I am a square")
    }
}
class Circle: Shape
{
    func identify()
    {
        println("I am a circle")
    }
}
```

Now, we define an array for storing shapes and then add some shapes to it:

```
var shapes = [Shape]()

let sq = Square()
let ci = Circle()

shapes.append(sq)
shapes.append(ci)
```

The array is defined to store generic shapes, but because both Circle and Square are subclasses of Shape, they too can be stored in the array.

With this structure in place, we now want to create a general-purpose function to do something with our array of shapes (e.g., drawing them on a display or calling some other subclass-specific method). As we walk through the array, we might want to know the type of each member (whether it's a circle or a square, or something else), but we might also want to be able to treat each member as its subclass type (rather than the generic type of the array) so that we can use features unique to each subclass. For that we can use the as and as? downcast operators.

The as operator forcibly downcasts to a specific subclass type. If the object you're trying to downcast is not actually of the specified class or is not a subclass of the specified class, Swift will terminate with a runtime error.

The as? operator attempts to downcast to a specific subclass type and returns an optional value. If the downcast fails (meaning that the object you're trying to downcast is not of the specified class or a subclass of the specified class), the value returned is nil. If the downcast succeeds, the returned value is the type to which it was downcast.

Suppose that we wanted to walk through our shape array searching for a specific type of entry. Even though we could do that by using the is operator, here's how we would do it using the as? operator and let binding:

```
for s in shapes
{
    if let c = s as? Circle
    {
        // c is now a reference to an array entry downcast
        // as a circle instead of as a generic shape
    }
    else
    {
        // downcast failed
    }
}
```

Alternatively, we could use a switch statement to achieve a similar goal:

```
for s in shapes
{
    switch s
    {
        case let cc as Circle:
            cc.identify()
        case let ss as Square:
            ss.describe()
        default:
            break;
    }
}
```

Note in the preceding example how we again use let binding so that we have a reference to the array entry, but the reference is cast to the subclass type so that cc refers to a Circle. This allows us to call methods unique to the Circle type, whereas ss refers to a Square, and lets us call methods unique to the square type.

If you're sure that a downcast won't fail and you don't want to use let binding, you can use the as operator to forcibly downcast from the generic class to the subclass like this:

```
for s in shapes
{
    if s is Circle
    {
        let c = s as Circle
        c.identify()
    }
}
```

Protocols

A protocol defines a standard set of features, expressed via properties, methods, operators, and subscripts, that embody a specific role or provide a specific set of functionality. A protocol isn't the implementation of this functionality; it just describes what must be implemented.

A class, structure, or enumeration can subsequently *adopt* the protocol, which implies that the class, structure, or enumeration will include its own definitions of the features that the protocol declares, thereby *conforming* to the protocol.

The syntax for declaring a new protocol is as follows:

```
protocol ProtocolName
{
    // protocol definition
}
```

NOTE

By convention, protocol names begin with an uppercase letter, and use camel case for the remainder of the protocol name.

The syntax for adopting one or more protocols is as follows:

```
class ClassName : [SuperClassName]
        ProtocolName [, ProtocolName…]
{
    // class definition and code that
    // implements the requirements of ProtocolName(s)
}
```

If the class is derived from an existing class, the superclass name appears before any protocol names.

The protocol body consists of a series of declarations that define the requirements that must be implemented in order for the adopter to conform to the protocol. This includes a list of the required properties and methods that the adopter must define and any constraints on them (e.g., whether a property is read-only or read/write).

Required Properties

A property requirement for a protocol specifies both the name of the property and its type as well as whether the property is read-only or read/write. It does not specify whether the property is implemented as a stored property or as a computed property, because that is up to the adopter.

You declare properties by using var in this fashion:

```
protocol SomeProtocol
{
    var aWritableProperty: Double { get set }
    var aReadOnlyProperty: Int { get }
    class var aTypeProperty: String { get set }
}
```

This example also demonstrates how the type of a property is specified and whether it must be implemented as a read-only property (by using just the get keyword) or read/write (by using both the get and set keywords).

To conform to this protocol, an adopter must define a read/write property named aWritableProperty, a read-only property named aReadOnlyProperty, and a read/write type property named aTypeProperty.

Note that the class keyword is used to indicate a type property, even if the protocol will be adopted by a structure or an enumeration.

Required Methods

A method requirement for a protocol specifies the name, parameters, and return type of the method. You write it in the same way as you would define an ordinary method in a class, except for the method body. This next example defines a protocol that requires adopters implement a method that returns a (presumably) printable string:

```
protocol aProtocol
{
    func printable() -> String
}
```

A class adopting this protocol must include a method that returns a printable representation of the instance.

A required method in a protocol can be an instance method (as shown in the example) or a type method (by preceding it with the keyword class).

If a required method needs to be able to mutate the instance that it refers to, precede it with the keyword mutating (see the subsection "Mutating Methods" on page 110 in "Structures" on page 108).

Optional Methods and Properties

You can use the keyword optional in front of a method or property name in a protocol to indicate that the method or property does not have to be implemented by a class that adopts that protocol.

There is an important restriction, though, in the use of the optional keyword: the protocol definition must be prefixed with the @objc keyword, even if there is no intention to interact with Objective-C code or data. This immediately places further restrictions on what you can do with the protocol, notably the following:

- @objc protocols can only be adopted by classes, not by structures or enumerations.

- You cannot use generic types in the protocol (using the typealias keyword, as described in the section "Generic Protocols" on page 154).

- You cannot use any Swift data type in the protocol that has no Objective-C equivalent (so, for example, the protocol cannot define anything that uses or requires a tuple).

The example that follows demonstrates a protocol that defines an optional property and an optional method. The property is defined as a read-only string (because only the get keyword is present), and the method is defined as taking an integer parameter, and returning an integer string:

```
@objc protocol Optionals
{
    optional var optProperty: String { get }
    optional func optMethod(i: Int) -> String
}
```

Next, we define two classes that each adopt the protocol. One class only implements the optional method; the other only implements the optional property:

```
class ImplementsProperty: Optionals
{
    let optProperty = "I'm a property!"
}

class ImplementsMethod: Optionals
{
    func optMethod(i: Int) -> String
    {
        return "I'm a method and was passed \(i)"
    }
}
```

Finally, we create an instance of each class to demonstrate how we access the optionally defined features. In doing so, note that the variables a and b are declared to be of type Optionals (the protocol), not of either of the class types:

```
var a: Optionals = ImplementsProperty()
var b: Optionals = ImplementsMethod()
```

Looking first at our instance a, you might expect that you can reference it directly, and, technically, you can:

```
a.optProperty
// returns an optional String? "I am a property!"
```

Notice, though, that the returned value is an optional string, even though the property is declared in the protocol as a non-optional string, and the class actually implements the property. Because optional methods and properties might not have been implemented in an adopting class, they *always* return an optional value. Thus, you must test for a non-nil value and then unwrap it to safely use the property value.

Because you can access the property, you might wonder what happens if you try to access the (unimplemented) method:

```
a.optMethod(1)
// compiler error
```

Rather than returning an optional value of nil, this code generates an error because the method hasn't actually been implemented. Instead, you must call the method with a question mark immediately following its name, as in this example:

```
a.optMethod?(1)
// returns nil
```

When called this way, we do get a nil value—in this case, indicating that the method has not been defined. Finally, let's consider our instance b, created earlier, that implements the optional method but not the optional property:

```
b.optMethod?(1)
// returns an optional String? "I am a method and was passed 1"

b.optProperty
// returns nil
```

This time, the method return (defined as a nonoptional string) is wrapped in an optional because the method implementation itself is optional, whereas the property, which has not been implemented, returns nil.

When a protocol is defined with an optional method or property, you can also use optional chaining to access the optional entities. See also the sections "Optionals" on page 63 and "Optional Chaining" on page 66 for more information.

Adopting Protocols with Extensions

Protocol use isn't limited to classes, structures, and enumerations that you define yourself: you can use Swift's extension mechanism to conform any existing type to a protocol, including simple built-in types such as Int, Double, and String.

The basic syntax for defining such an extension is as follows:

```
extension Type : ProtocolName [, ProtocolName…]
{
    // code that extends Type and implements
    // the requirements of ProtocolName(s)
}
```

Following is an example of using an extension to conform the
Bool type to the Printable protocol that we introduced earlier.
This example is somewhat contrived because the global print
function will print Bool types as either "true" or "false", so we
define our implementation to print "YES" and "NO" instead:

```
extension Bool: Printable
{
    func printable() -> String
    {
        return self ? "YES":"NO"
    }
}
```

Here's how to use this with Bool types:

```
var a = false
a.printable()
// returns "NO"
```

Inheritance and Protocols

In the same way that you can use inheritance with classes, you
can use inheritance with protocols—one protocol inherits all of
the requirements of another and then adds further requirements of its own.

The syntax for basing one protocol on another is as follows:

```
protocol ProtocolName : ProtocolName [, ProtocolName…]
{
    // protocol definition
}
```

The next example demonstrates a simple protocol that requires
that adopters implement the method asHex() to return a hex
representation of the type, but because it inherits from the
Printable protocol (described earlier), adopters must also
implement a method named printable():

```
protocol Hexable : Printable
{
    func asHex() -> String
}
```

And here, we define an extension to the Bool type that adopts
the Hexable protocol and implements the required methods:

```
extension Bool: Hexable
{
    func asHex() -> String
    {
        return self ? "1":"0"
    }

    func printable() -> String
    {
        return self ? "YES":"NO"
    }

}
```

NOTE

For the purpose of demonstration, we'll assume that the
reader is happy to forgive the contrivance that "1" is the
hex equivalent of true, and that "0" is the hex equivalent of
false.

Using a Protocol as a Type

A protocol is a type in the same way that a class is a type, and
you can use protocols in most places that you can use types.
This is a hugely powerful feature, especially when you begin to
think of types not in terms of what they can store (Ints,
Strings, *data*) but in terms of the functionality that they can
provide (methods, actions, *conformed behavior*).

With this mindset, we can think of a variable not as a place to
store a specific type of value but as a place to store anything
that implements specific *behavior*. Similarly, we can think of an

array not as a place to store a collection of one type of data but as a place to store a collection of *anything* that implements a specific behavior.

Earlier, we demonstrated an extension to the Bool type that adopted the Hexable protocol. Here's a similar extension for the UInt type:

```
extension UInt: Hexable
{
    func asHex() -> String
    {
        var temp = self
        var result = ""
        let digits = Array("0123456789abcdef")
        digits
        while (temp > 0)
        {
            result = String(digits[Int(temp &
                         0x0f)]) + result
            temp >>= 4
        }
        return result
    }

    func printable() -> String
    {
        return "\(self)"
    }

}
```

With both Bool and UInt conforming to the Hexable protocol, we can now create some interesting behavior with variables:

```
var a: Hexable = true
a.printable()    // returns "YES"
a.asHex()        // returns "1"
a = 45
a.printable()    // returns "45"
a.asHex()        // returns "2d"
```

The variable a is of type Hexable; it can store anything that conforms to the Hexable protocol, which means it can store both Bool and UInt data.

This next example defines an array of type `Hexable`, and populates it with some values:

```
var ar = [Hexable]()
ar.append(true)
ar.append(45)
ar[0].asHex()    // returns "1"
ar[1].asHex()    // returns "2d"
```

Again, the array is not limited to being able to store just `Bool` data or just `UInt` data: it can store `Hexable` data, which, due to protocol conformance, includes both `Bool` and `UInt` types.

Checking Protocol Conformance

You can use the `is`, `as`, and `as?` type casting operators to check for protocol conformance and to downcast protocols in the same way that you can use them to check and downcast class types, because you can define protocols in terms of other protocols (inheritance) in the same way that you can define classes in terms of other classes.

There is an important restriction, though, in the use of these operators in checking and downcasting protocols: the protocol definition must be prefixed with the `@objc` keyword, even if there is no intention to interact with Objective-C code or data. This is the same restriction that was described earlier in the section "Optional Methods and Properties" on page 134, and it imposes the same limitations when checking for protocol conformance.

The `@objc` keyword requirement also means that you cannot check if an instance conforms to a built-in Swift protocol, because those protocols aren't defined with the `@objc` keyword.

If you can work within these restrictions, you can use the type checking and downcasting operators in the same way that you would use types. For example, the following defines a sample protocol, class, and general function to check if any instance conforms to the protocol using the `is` keyword:

```
@objc protocol DemoProto
{
}

class DemoClass: DemoProto
{
}

func protoCheck(t: AnyObject) -> Bool
{
    return t is DemoProto
}
```

Next, we create some objects that we then pass to the protocol checking function:

```
var s = DemoClass()
var a = 4
protoCheck(s)  // returns true
protoCheck(a)  // returns false
```

The instance of s returns true because s is an instance of Demo Class, which adopts the DemoProto protocol.

Built-In Protocols

There are many built-in protocols in Swift: some are used to define the language itself, while others are useful to adopt for your own classes so that you can use them in many of the same contexts as Swift's built-in types.

Table 7 lists some of the more useful among them.

Table 7. Built-in protocols

Protocol	Description
AbsoluteValuable	For types that support the abs (absolute value) function.
Comparable	For types that can be magnitude-compared using relational operators like < and ==.
Equatable	For types that can be compared for equality using == and != .

Protocol	Description
ForwardIndexType	For types that can represent discrete values in a series, and that implement the successor() method to step from one value to the next.
Hashable	For types that can provide an integer hash value and can be used as keys in a dictionary.
Printable	For types that can be converted to a text representation and written to an output stream (such as by println).
SignedNumberType	For types that can be subtracted, negated, or initialized from 0.
Streamable	For types that can be written to an output stream (such as String, Character, and UnicodeScalar)
Strideable	For types that can represent a continuous sequence of values that can be offset and measured.

If you are interested in implementing these protocols, or exploring any other aspects of Swift, open a playground or any Swift source file and locate (or just type in) the global function name println. Next, Command-Option-click this function name, and the assistant editor will open the equivalent of a "Swift Header File," which defines and document's many aspects of the language. You'll need to do this to see what features must be added to your own class so that it conforms to each protocol.

Memory Management

Swift, like Objective-C, uses *reference counting* as the main technique for keeping track of when dynamically allocated memory is no longer being used and can be released for other purposes.

For many years, Objective-C used (and can still use) manual reference counting, but this requires diligence on the part of the developer, and even though it can obviously be mastered, it is a challenge for those new to the language to understand the nuances of when to use certain methods associated with reference counting, and when not to use them.

After a brief experiment with an Objective-C garbage collector for automatic memory management, Apple announced ARC in 2011. ARC—which stands for Automatic Reference Counting —uses the same approach that a programmer would use, but it does so in a rigorous and deterministic manner.

How Reference Counting Works

The principle underpinning reference counting is quite simple. Every object (that is, every instance of a class) has a built-in *reference count* property that is set to 1 when the object is instantiated.

Whenever a piece of code wants to express an interest in or ownership over the object (that is, when a pointer is created that points to the object), it must increment the reference counter. When it has finished with the object and has no further interest in it (that is, when its pointer to the object is no longer needed), it must decrement the reference counter. (In Objective-C, the way to express interest in an object is to call its retain method, and the way to express no further interest is to call the object's release method.)

When the reference counter for an object is decremented to zero, it means that there are no current references to the object and that the object can be destroyed and the memory allocated to it can be released.

As long as an object's instantiation and release happens in the one function, the process of reference counting is very simple to master. The intricacies of reference counting don't really become apparent until the instantiation of an object is disconnected (code or execution-wise) from its release. At this point, it is relatively easy for a novice programmer to not release an object to which they created a reference (which results in a memory leak) or to release an object that they don't actually own (which can result in a crash).

ARC manages the entire process of reference counting, automatically determining where to add retain and release calls, and thus relieves the programmer from the responsibility of doing so.

Retain Cycles and Strong References

One of the main problems with a reference counting approach to memory management is that of *retain cycles*. At their simplest, these occur when two objects contain *strong references* to each other. Consider the following code:

```
class A { }
var a = A()
```

The variable a stores a strong reference to the newly created instance of class A.

Strong references are also created by default when objects store references to each other. This next example has been trimmed to the bare minimum, but this situation can occur in many places where complex interlinked data structures are used:

```
class A
{
    var otherObject: B?
}

class B
{
    var otherObject: A?
}

var a = A() // retain count for new instance of A set to 1
var b = B() // retain count for new instance of B set to 1
a.otherObject = b
// B instance retain count incremented to 2
b.otherObject = a
// A instance retain count incremented to 2
```

The code demonstrates two instances, referred to by `a` and `b`, that also refer to each other. After this code has executed, the retain count for each of the instances will be 2.

When the section of code that instantiates these two classes goes out of scope, `a` and `b`, being local variables, also go out of scope and are deleted. When `a` is deleted, the retain count for the instance it refers to is decremented (to 1), but because it is not zero, the instance itself is not deleted. Similarly, when `b` is deleted, the retain count for the instance it refers to is decremented (again, to 1), but, again, because it is not zero, that instance is also not deleted.

As a consequence, we end up with two instances (one of class A, one of class B) that refer to each other and thus keep each other "alive." Because the retain count for both instances never reaches zero, neither object can be deleted, and both take up memory.

This situation is a referred to as a *memory leak*, and if the situation that created it occurs repeatedly during the execution of the program, the amount of memory allocated to the program will continue to grow, possibly causing performance issues or termination by the operating system if it limits the amount of memory that an application can claim.

Although retain cycles are something that an experienced coder might consider when manually managing memory, they are not something that ARC can prevent without some assistance from the programmer. Essentially, if ARC is to manage memory automatically, it requires some additional information about the nature of references to other objects—they need to be classified as either *weak* or *unowned*.

Weak References

One way to prevent a retain cycle is to change one of the strong references to a weak reference. You do this by preceding the `var` declaration with the keyword `weak`, as in this example:

```
class A
{
    var otherObject: B?
}

class B
{
    weak var otherObject: A?
}
```

Weak references have two effects:

- There is no assertion that the referrer "owns" the instance it refers to, and it can deal with the fact that the instance might go away (in practical terms, this means that when a weak reference is established, the retain count is not incremented).

- When an instance referred to by a weak reference is deallocated, ARC sets the weak reference value to nil (thus, weak references must be declared as variables, not constants).

With a weak reference in place, consider in this next example how the retain counts change as the code executes:

```
var a = A() // retain count for new instance of A set to 1
var b = B() // retain count for new instance of B set to 1
a.otherObject = b
// B instance retain count incremented to 2
b.otherObject = a
// A instance retain count remains at 1
```

Because the reference that the instance of B holds to A is a weak reference, the retain count for the A instance remains at 1.

As before, when the local variables a and b go out of scope and are deleted, the retain count for the instances they refer to are both decremented. That means that the retain count for the instance of A drops to zero, and the retain count for the instance of B drops to 1.

Because the instance of A now has a retain count of zero, it is no longer required in memory, and the process of its deinitialization and deallocation can begin. During deallocation, two things to happen:

- The weak reference to the instance of A that is stored in the instance of B is set to nil.

- Because the instance of A holds a strong reference to the instance of B (and A is being deallocated), the deallocation process sends B a release message, decrementing its retain count to zero.

At this point, the instance of A has been removed from memory, and we are left with an instance of B that has a retain count of zero. The process of its deinitialization and deallocation now begins.

When using weak references, consider the following:

- Use a weak reference if your code and data model allows for a reference to have no value (i.e., be nil) at times during the execution of your program.

- Weak references must always be defined as optionals.

Unowned References

An unowned reference is similar to a weak reference in that there is no assertion that the referrer "owns" the instance to which it refers, and when an unowned reference is established, the instance's retain count is not incremented.

The main difference between a weak reference and an unowned reference is that whereas a weak reference may at times validly be nil without causing errors, an unowned reference, once established, must always have a value.

An unowned reference is defined by preceding the var declaration with the keyword unowned, as in this example:

```
class B
{
    unowned var otherObject: A
}
```

When using unowned references, consider the following:

- Use an unowned reference if your code or data model expects that the reference, after creation, will always exist and be valid (at least until such time as the referrer goes out of scope or is deleted).

- Unowned references must always be defined as nonoptionals.

- If you try to access an instance that has been deallocated via an unowned reference, Swift will terminate with a runtime error.

Retain Cycles and Closures

Like classes, closures are actually reference types. If you assign a closure to a property of an instance and that closure captures the instance, either by reference to a property of the instance or by a method call on the instance, you will have created a retain cycle between the instance and the closure.

The solution to this is to use either a weak or an unowned reference in the closure to the instance or method that is being captured, but the syntax is not the same as for references, as described earlier. Instead, references are specified in a *capture list* as part of the definition of the closure.

A capture list is defined inside the closure definition either immediately prior to the parameter list or immediately prior to the in keyword if the closure has no parameters. The capture list is a series of one or more reference types (unowned or weak, followed by the property or method that it refers to) and separated by commas, as follows:

```
{
    [referenceType propertyOrMethod [, ...] ]
    (parameters) -> returnType in
        statements
}
```

For example, a closure being stored in a property aClosure, and referencing self, would look as follows:

```
var aClosure: (parameters) -> returnType =
{
    [unowned self]
    (parameters) -> returnType in
        statements
}
```

The rules as to which type of reference you should use remain the same as they do for instance-to-instance references. Use a weak reference (defined as an optional) if the reference may validly become nil; use an unowned reference if the closure and the instance that it captures refer to each other, and the reference will remain valid until both objects can be deallocated.

Generics

Swift's *generics* feature provides you with the ability to write generic code that can work with any type of data. Similar features exist in C++ (as *templates*) and C# (as *generics*). Parts of the Swift standard library are implemented as generics. For example, the Array type and the Dictionary type are generic collections that can store any type of data.

In Swift, you can write generic code in a number of ways, including generic functions, generic types, and generic protocols.

Generic Functions

To see a classic example of where generics are useful, consider the Swift standard library function swap, which is defined as follows:

```
func swap<T>(inout a: T, inout b: T)
```

From this function definition, we can see swap takes two inout parameters, of some type T, but there's nothing to indicate what type T actually is. (The two parameters are declared as inout parameters because the function must swap two existing items, not copies of them.)

swap is a generic function that can swap a pair of Ints, Doubles, or even a pair of instances of a user-defined type. It can swap any two variables, as long as they are of the same type. To get a better understanding of what swap is doing, take a look at this next example to consider how it would be implemented:

```
func swap<T>(inout a: T, inout b: T)
{
    let temp = a
    a = b
    b = temp
}
```

Nothing in the body of the function definition is type specific. So long as the constant temp is of the same type as a (which it will be due to type inferencing), and a is of the same type as b (which it must be according to the types specified in the parameter list of the function), this function can swap any two same-typed values.

You define generic functions by using the following syntax:

```
func someFunc<Placeholder, [Placeholder...]>(parameterList)
{
    // function body
}
```

The key parts of the definition that indicate that this is a generic function are the angle brackets immediately following the function name; these contains one or more *type placeholders*. These placeholders, called *type parameters*, stand in for actual types throughout the body of the function.

In much the same way that "i" has become a *defacto* loop variable, "T" is commonly used as the name for a type parameter in generic functions, but you can use any valid identifier.

By convention, type identifiers begin with an uppercase letter, and use camel case for the remainder of the identifier name.

Generic Types

Earlier in this book, in the section "Arrays" on page 42, it was noted that the preferred way to refer to an array of a specific type is [*SomeType*], but that the formal way is Array<*SomeType*>. The angle brackets reveal that the Array type is actually implemented as a generic type, and you can create our own generic types in the same way, using classes, structures, or enumerations.

This next example is a generic struct-based implementation of a queue:

```
struct Queue<T>
{
    var entries = [T]()

    mutating func enqueue(item: T)
    {
        entries.append(item)
    }

    mutating func dequeue() -> T
    {
        return entries.removeAtIndex(0)
    }
}
```

The queued data is stored in an array, entries, of type T, and defines two methods: enqueue (to add an item to the end of the queue) and dequeue (to pull an item from the beginning of the queue).

So defined, Queue is now a new, generic type, and you can create queues for integers, strings, and any other data type to

which you have access. For example, you can create and use a
queue for Int data as follows:

```
var q = Queue<Int>()
q.enqueue(45)
q.enqueue(39)
q.enqueue(61)
q.enqueue(98)
q
// returns 45, 39, 61, 98
q.dequeue()
// returns 45
q
// returns 39, 61, 98
```

Constraining Types

In designing a generic function or type, you might want to
place some limits on what types it can support. You can constrain types based on either their class (or subclass) or by protocol conformance. The constraint is specified in the angle
brackets immediately following the type parameter you want to
constrain, as follows:

```
<T: SomeClass>
<T: SomeProtocol>
```

In the first example, T can act only as a placeholder for instances of SomeClass (or its subclasses). In the second example, T
can act only as a placeholder for types that conform to the
specified protocol.

Revisiting our Queue example from earlier, we could constrain
it to support only signed integer as follows:

```
struct Queue<T: SignedIntegerType>
{
    // existing definition
}
```

SignedIntegerType is a protocol built into Swift that the signed
integer types (Int, Int8, Int16, Int32, and Int64) conform to,
but which the unsigned types (UInt, UInt8, etc.) do not.

With this constraint in place, we can no longer create a queue for UInt data:

```
var q = Queue<UInt>()
// error - Type 'UInt' does not conform to
// protocol 'SignedIntegerType'
```

The example that follows is a generic function that can merge two sorted arrays into a third. Because this function compares entries from each array, we need to be sure that comparison is a defined operation for the type of data stored in the arrays, and we do that by constraining the type T to the Comparable protocol. Types that conform to this protocol can be compared with the relational operators <, <=, >= and >, and Swift's built-in types (such as Double, Int, and String) all conform:

```
func merge<T:Comparable>(a:[T], b:[T]) -> [T]
{
    var output = [T]()
    var i = 0, j = 0

    let sizea = a.count
    let sizeb = b.count
    output.reserveCapacity(sizea + sizeb)

    while (i < sizea) && (j < sizeb)
    {
        if a[i] < b[j] { output.append(a[i++]) }
        else { output.append(b[j++]) }
    }

    while i < sizea { output.append(a[i++]) }
    while j < sizeb { output.append(b[j++]) }

    return output
}
```

Here's a simple example of using our merge function with strings:

```
let s = ["allan", "fred", "mike"]
let t = ["brenda", "geraldine", "ruth"]
let u = merge(s, t)
u
// returns "allan", "brenda", "fred", "geraldine",
// "mike", "ruth"
```

Generic Protocols

With Swift, you can also write generic protocols, although the way this works is a little different to the way generic types are expressed in function and type definitions. Instead of a <T> placeholder, unknown types in protocols are identified by using the typealias keyword, which we introduced early on in the section "Types" on page 17. When you use them in this way in protocol definitions, these are known as *associated types*.

To use an associated type, the protocol definition takes this form:

```
protocol SomeProtocol
{
    typealias SomeName
    // remainder of protocol definition with the generic
    // type references expressed as SomeName
}
```

The actual type that the type alias *SomeName* refers to is defined when the protocol is adopted, in the same way that the other required parts of the protocol must be defined to provide conformance:

```
class SomeClass : SomeProtocol
{
    typealias SomeName = SomeActualType
    // rest of class definition
}
```

Here's an example of a generic protocol, Queueable, that demonstrates the use of an associated type:

```
protocol Queueable
{
    typealias NativeType
    mutating func enqueue(item: NativeType)
    mutating func dequeue() -> NativeType
}
```

A class or structure that adopts this protocol must implement enqueue and dequeue methods (thus, behaving like a queue), but the type of data that these methods use is defined in the adopting class at the same place that the methods themselves are defined—in the protocol definition, it's referred to as NativeType.

Following is an example of a structure that stores a list of strings and adopts the Queueable protocol so that the list can also be treated as a queue. You can see that the NativeType from the protocol is defined as being of String type for this particular adopter:

```
struct StringList: Queueable
{
    var list = [String]()

    typealias NativeType = String

    mutating func enqueue(item: NativeType)
    {
        list.append(item)
    }

    mutating func dequeue() -> NativeType
    {
        return list.removeAtIndex(0)
    }
}
```

You could use the structure as follows:

```
var s = StringList()
s.enqueue("Joshua")
s.enqueue("Nadia")
s.enqueue("Paul")
s.dequeue()
// returns "Joshua"
s
// returns an array ["Nadia", "Paul"]
```

Operator Overloading

Operator overloading is the ability to define custom behavior for standard operators (+, /, =, etc.) when they are used with custom types. Overloading is a controversial feature because it can lead to ambiguous code.

For example, all programmers understand that the + operator is traditionally associated with addition when both operands are numeric. A slightly smaller group generally associate + with concatenation when both operands are strings, so in a sense, + is already overloaded in languages that support concatenation with it.

A language that supports programmer-defined operator overloading takes this further, allowing the programmer to add new custom behavior to any of the standard operators when they are applied to custom types. For example, you could define a struct type to represent vectors. Adding vectors is a natural operation for people who think in terms of motion, and overloading + to add two vector types allows vector addition to be expressed naturally in code.

You overload binary infix operators in Swift by using the following syntax:

```
func + ([inout] left: SomeType, right: SomeType)
    -> SomeType
{
    // code that returns a value of SomeType
}
```

Let's look closer at this syntax:

- The parameter names are shown as left and right, but you can use any other parameter names. The first parameter is the one that appears on the lefthand side of the operator, and the second parameter is the one that appears on the righthand side.

- This example overloads +, but you can overload any existing binary operator (including compound assignment operators and comparison operators) except for assignment (=).

- When overloading compound assignment operators (such as +=), the first (left) parameter must be prefixed with inout because the body of the function will directly modify the left parameter.

- The two input types are both shown as *SomeType*, but these do not have to be of the same type.

- The return value does not have to be the same type as either of the operands.

Back in the section "Structures" on page 108, we introduced a simple structure named Rect to represent rectangular shapes, as shown in this example:

```
struct Rect
{
    var x = 0.0, y = 0.0, width = 0.0, height = 0.0

    func area() -> Double
    {
        return (width * height)
    }
}
```

Here is an overloaded version of the + operator that returns a new Rect that represents the smallest Rect that would contain the two operand Rects (assuming the origin is at the upper left):

```
func + (left: Rect, right: Rect) -> Rect
{
    return Rect (
                    x: min(left.x, right.x),
                    y: min(left.y, right.y),
                    width: max(left.width, right.width),
                    height: max(left.height, right.height)
                )
}
```

We would use this new operator as follows:

```
var a = Rect (x:5, y:5, width:5, height:5)
var b = Rect (x:6, y:6, width:10, height:10)
var c = a + b
// c is now a Rect where
// (x=5.0, y=5.0, width=10.0, height=10.0)
```

The following example overloads the < operator so that two Rects can be compared in terms of area:

```
func < (left: Rect, right: Rect) -> Bool
{
    return left.area() < right.area()
}
```

You could use this as follows:

```
var e = Rect(x:0, y:0, width:4, height:5)
var f = Rect(x:5, y:5, width:5, height:5)
e<f
// returns true
```

Overloading Unary Operators

The unary operators are overloaded by preceding the function definition with either the prefix or postfix keyword. The general pattern is as follows:

```
prefix func ++ (someName: someType) -> someType
{
    // code that returns a value of SomeType
}
```

Here's an alternative:

```
postfix func -- (someName: someType) -> someType
{
    // code that returns a value of SomeType
}
```

The parameter names are shown as *someName*, but you can use any parameter names.

Note that the return value does not have to be the same type as the operand.

The following example defines a ++ postfix operator for our Rect type that adds 1.0 to the x- and y-coordinates but leaves the width and height unmodified:

```
postfix func ++ (inout r: Rect) -> Rect
{
    let temp = r;
    r.x += 1.0
    r.y += 1.0
    return temp
}
```

Note that this function copies the operand so that the value returned is the original, unmodified value (thus mimicking the expected behavior of a postfix ++ operator). In use, this would behave as follows:

```
var d = Rect(x:5, y:5, width:5, height:5)
d++
// returns a Rect where
// (x=5.0, y=5.0, width=5.0, height=5.0)
// but d is a Rect where
// (x=6.0, y=6.0, width=5.0, height=5.0)
```

Custom Operators

As well as overloading the built-in operators, you can create custom operators which can begin with any of the ASCII characters +, -, *, /, =, !, %, <, >, &, |, ^, and ~, as well as a range of Unicode character blocks, including the math, symbol, arrow, dingbat, line drawing, and box drawing sets. The second and subsequent characters can be any of those listed as well as the any of the Unicode combining characters (which are characters that modify other characters, such as diacritical marks and accents).

Unusually, custom operators in Swift need to be declared before they are defined, using this syntax:

```
[prefix|postfix|infix] operator symbols {}
```

For example, we could declare a prefix operator that used the square root symbol ($\sqrt{}$) to calculate square roots, as follows:

```
prefix operator √ {}
```

We could then implement it thus:

```
prefix func √ (operand: Double) -> Double
{
    return sqrt(operand)
}
```

So defined, we can then use our operator as follows:

```
print (√25)
// outputs 5.0
```

Custom Operator Precedence

When you define custom infix operators, you can also specify optional precedence and associativity values. These values are specified when the custom operator is declared (not when it is subsequently defined) as follows:

```
operator symbols { associativity someValue
                   precedence someValue }
```

Precedence is specified as a numeric value, and defaults to 100 if not provided.

Associativity is specified as left, right, or none, and defaults to none if not provided.

See also the subsection "Operator Precedence" on page 36 in "Operators" on page 29 for more information.

Ranges, Intervals, and Strides

Earlier in this book, we introduced the closed range operator $(x...y)$ and the half-open range operator $(x..<y)$. These operators represent two of the more commonly used types of ranges (they're used frequently in iteration), but Swift supports two other range types: *intervals* and *strides*.

Let's look at all three of these types a little more closely.

Ranges

A range is a collection of consecutive discrete values. The end of the range must be reachable from the start by a process of repeated incrementation (so the start can't be a value that is later in the series than the end).

Typically, you will use ranges with integer types, but you can use them with any type that conforms to the ForwardIndexType protocol.

Ranges are types (so, for example, a variable can be of type range) and include the properties startIndex and endIndex, as demonstrated in this example:

```
var r = 1...5
r
// returns "1..<6"
r.startIndex
// returns 1
r.endIndex
// returns 6

for x in r
{
    println (x)
}
// outputs:
// 1
// 2
// 3
// 4
// 5
```

Observe that even though we assigned the closed range 1...5 to r, Swift converted this internally to the half-open range 1..<6. This is because it always represents ranges internally in half-open format.

The endIndex represents the end of a range but is not a value in the range, which is why the for loop only outputs five values.

Intervals

Like a range, an interval consists of a start value and an end value, and the start must be less than the end, but intervals are not associated with indexing or the concept of advancing progressively from the start to the end by incrementation. Instead, they are associated with the idea of *containment*—checking whether a value is contained within the interval.

You can use intervals with any type that conforms to the Comparable protocol. Thus, intervals can be of type Int or Double, or any other type that conforms to that protocol.

Intervals are types (so a variable can be of type interval) and include the properties start and end as well as the method contains(), as demonstrated in this example:

```
var i = 1.1...2.2
i.start
// returns 1.1
i.end
// returns 2.2
i.contains(3.4)
// returns false
i.contains(1.6)
// returns true
i.contains(2.2)
// returns true
```

Like ranges, you can define intervals as either half-open or closed.

When a type used with the half-open or closed range operator conforms to only the Comparable protocol (such as the floating-point types) the operator will always return an interval.

However, if a type used with either of the range operators conforms to both the Comparable and ForwardIndexType protocols (such as the integer types), the operator will return an interval when it is used in a pattern matching context (e.g., a switch case), but it will return a range in any other context.

Strides

Like ranges and intervals, a stride consists of a start and an end, but it also includes a distance to step as the sequence progresses.

The end value of a stride can be inclusive (specified with the through parameter name) or exclusive (specified with the to parameter name).

Unlike ranges and intervals, none of these values are accessible as properties of the stride.

You can use strides with any type that conforms to the `Strideable` protocol, which includes floating-point and integer types.

Strides are types, so a variable can be of type `stride`, as in the following example:

```
var s = stride(from:2, to:8, by:2)
for x in s
{
    println (x)
}
// outputs
// 2
// 4
// 6
```

Because the stride in the previous example was initialized with a `to` parameter, the end value of the stride (8) was excluded from the sequence. In this next example, we use a stride directly, but this time we initialize it by using the `through` parameter so that the end value (2.8) is included in the sequence:

```
for x in stride(from:2.2, through:2.8, by:0.3)
{
    println (x)
}
// outputs
// 2.2
// 2.5
// 2.8
```

Note that due to the inability to exactly represent all floating-point values, a stride initialized with a floating-point `to` parameter may appear to return the end value as the last value in a sequence. This is not an issue with strides, but a reminder that floating-point values should not be relied on for certain values.

Global Functions

Swift includes many built-in global functions, some of which have been used as examples in earlier parts of this book. The more useful functions are listed in this section, along with a brief discussion of their parameter requirements and what they do.

If you are interested in further exploring the global function documentation, open a playground or any Swift source file and locate (or just type in) the global function name `println`. Next, Command-Option-click this function name, which opens the assistant editor equivalent of a "Swift Header File." This defines and documents many aspects of the language.

`advancedBy(n: Distance)`

> This is not a global function per se, but it is a method that is implemented for built-in types conforming to the `Strideable` protocol. It returns the result of applying `successor()` or `predecessor()` to self n times. For example, `5.advancedBy(2)` returns 7.

`abs(x)`

> Returns the absolute value of x, which must conform to the `AbsoluteValuable` protocol.

`assert(condition: Bool, message: String)`

> Tests the `condition`. If it evaluates to `false`, it terminates the program and prints the string `message` as an error.

`distanceTo(other: Self)`

> This is not a global function per se, but it is a method that is implemented for built-in types conforming to the `Strideable` protocol. It returns the number of times that `successor()` or `predecessor()` would need to be called to reach `other` from self. For example, `5.distanceTo(8)` returns 3.

`countElements(x)`

> Returns a count of the number of elements in x, which must conform to the `CollectionType` protocol (this includes strings, arrays, and dictionaries).

`isEmpty(x)`

> Returns a `Bool` indicating whether x is empty. x must conform to the `CollectionType` protocol, which includes strings, arrays, and dictionaries.

`last(x)`

> Returns an optional—either the last element of x, or `nil` if x is empty. x must conform to the `CollectionType` protocol.

`max(list)`

> Returns the greatest argument in the list. The list of comma-separated arguments must be of the same type, and must conform to the `Comparable` protocol, which includes `Ints` and `Doubles` (and their variants), and `Strings`.

`maxElement(x)`

> Returns the maximum element in x, which must be a collection (such as a `String` or `Array`) of a type that conforms to the `Comparable` protocol. This includes `Ints` and `Doubles` (and their variants), and `Strings`.

`min(list)`

> Returns the lesser argument passed. The list of comma-separated arguments must be of the same type, and must conform to the `Comparable` protocol, which includes `Ints` and `Doubles` (and their variants), and `Strings`.

`minElement(x)`

> Returns the minimum element in x, which must be a collection (such as a `String` or `Array`) of a type that conforms to the `Comparable` protocol. This includes `Ints` and `Doubles` (and their variants), and `Strings`.

`predecessor()`

> This is not a global function per se, but it is a method that is implemented for many built-in types, and returns the predecessor for the object that it is applied to. For example, `5.predecessor()` returns 4.

`print(x)`

> Writes the textual representation of x to the output stream.

`println(x)`

> Writes the textual representation of x to the output stream, followed by a new line.

`removeAll(&x [, keepCapacity:Bool])`

> Removes all elements from x, which must be specified by reference, and which must conform to the RangeRe placeableCollectionType protocol. This includes Strings and Arrays. If the keepCapacity parameter is specified and true, the space allocated to the collection will not be released.

`removeAtIndex(&x, i: IndexType)`

> Removes a single element at i from x, which must be specified by reference, and which must conform to the RangeReplaceableCollectionType protocol, which includes the String and Array types.

`removeLast(&x)`

> Removes the last element from x, which must be specified by reference, and which must conform to the RangeReplaceableCollectionType protocol, which includes Strings and Arrays.

`removeRange(&x, r: range)`

> Removes the range of elements from x, which must be specified by reference, and which must conform to the RangeReplaceableCollectionType protocol, which includes the String and Array types.

`reverse(x)`

> Returns a new array containing the elements of x in reverse order.

`sort(&x)`

> Sorts the collection x, which must be specified by reference, in place. x must conform to the MutableCollec tionType protocol and have an index that conforms to

the `RandomAccessIndexType` protocol. The elements must conform to the `Comparable` protocol. This includes `Array`s.

`sort(&x, { closure } )`

Sorts the array `x`, which must be specified by reference, in place. The closure defines how two elements sort with respect to each other (e.g., `{ $0<$1 }`). See the section "Closures" on page 57 for more information.

`sorted(x)`

Returns a sorted version of `x`, which must conform to the `SequenceType` protocol (this includes `Array`s) and have elements that conform to the `Comparable` protocol (which includes `Int`s, `Double`s, and their related types, and `String`s).

`sorted(x, { closure } )`

Returns a sorted version of `x`, which must conform to the `SequenceType` protocol (this includes `Array`s). The closure defines how two elements sort with respect to each other, (e.g., `{ $0<$1 }`). See the section "Closures" on page 57 for more information.

`split(x, { closure } )`

Returns the result of slicing `x`, which must conform to the `Sliceable` protocol (this includes `String`s and `Array`s). The closure defines where to split: for example, `{ $0 == " " }` could be used to split a string at a space character into an array of strings, or `{ $0 == 36 }` could be used to split an array of integers into an array of arrays of integers, splitting at every element in `x` that has the value 36. Optional parameters that follow the closure are `maxSplit` (an `Int` that limits the number of splits), and `allowEmptySlices` (a `Bool` that if `true` will cause a split for consecutive closure matches). See also the section "Closures" on page 57 for more information.

successor()

This is not a global function per se, but it is a method that is implemented for many built-in types, and returns the successor for the object that it is applied to. For example, 5.successor() returns 6.

swap(&x, &y)

Swaps x and y, which must be of the same type.

toString(x)

Returns the result of x printed as a String.

Index

Symbols
! exclamation mark
    as logical operator, 34
    custom operators and, 159
    unwrapping optionals and, 64
!= comparison operator, 33
    strings, 40
!== comparison operator, 33
character, 91
#include statements, 15
% percent sign, 159
%= assignment operator, 32
& operator (bitwise AND), 31
    custom operators and, 159
&% overflow remainder operator, 34
&& logical operator, 34
&* overflow multiplication operator, 34
&+ overflow addition operator, 34
&- overflow subtraction operator, 34
&/ overflow division operator, 34
&= assignment operator, 33
(double quotes), 19
* operator, 30

custom operators and, 159
*= assignment operator, 32
+ operator, 30
    custom operators and, 159
    string concatenation, 15
++ operator, 31
+= assignment operator, 32
- operator, 30
    custom operators and, 159
-- operator (decrement), 31
-= assignment operator, 32
-> closure expression, 57
..< half-open range operator, 35
/ operator, 30
    custom operators and, 159
/* */ (multi-line comment delimiter), 14
// (comment marker), 14
/= assignment operator, 32
; (semicolons), 14
< comparison operator, 33
    custom operators and, 159
    strings, 40
<< operator (bitwise left-shift), 31
<<= assignment operator, 32
<= comparison operator, 34
    strings, 40

= assignment operator, 32
    custom operators and, 159
= comparison operator, 34
== comparison operator, 33
    strings, 40
=== comparison operator, 33
> comparison operator, 34
    custom operators and, 159
    strings, 40
>= comparison operator, 34
    strings, 40
>> operator (bitwise right-shift), 32
>>= assignment operator, 32
? (question mark), 63
[] syntax
    for arrays, 43
    for dictionaries, 47-50
\" (double quote) escape sequence, 41
\' (single quote) escape sequence, 41
\n (line feed) escape sequence, 41
\r (carriage return) escape sequence, 41
\t (tab) escape sequence, 41
\u{n} arbitrary Unicode scalar escape sequence, 41
\\ (backslash) escape sequence, 41
^ operator
    bitwise XOR, 31
    custom operators and, 159
^= assignment operator, 33
_ underscore character, 78, 92
` (back ticks), 23
| operator
    bitwise OR, 31
    custom operators and, 159
|= assignment operator, 33
|| logical operator, 34
~ operator
    bitwise NOT, 31
    custom operators and, 159

… range operator, 35
√ (square root), 159

A

abs(x) global function, 164
AbsoluteValuable protocol, 141, 164
access control, 119-123
    default, 121-123
    of class members, 95
    specifying level of, 120
advancedBy() global function, 164
Any keyword, 127
AnyObject keyword, 127
Apple Worldwide Developers Conference, 1
ARC, 1
arguments, automatic names, 59
arithmetic operators, 30
arrays, 42-47
    algorithms for, 46
    append function, 44
    appending two, 44
    assigning value to element, 44
    assigning value to range of elements, 44
    capacity property, 43
    capacity, reserving, 45
    count property, 44
    elements, accessing, 43
    filter(), 46
    inserting values into, 44
    isEmpty property, 44
    iterating over, 45
    map(), 46
    modifying, 44-45
    mutable, 44-45
    mutable, declaring, 42
    properties of, 43
    reduce(), 46
    remove and return last element of, 45

remove and return single elements from, 44
removing all elements from, 44
reverse(), 47
sorted(), 47
sorting, 45
as operator, 127
    checking for protocol conformance, 140
    downcasting with, 130
as? operator, 35, 127
    checking for protocol conformance, 140
    downcasting with, 130
assignment operators, 32-33
associated types, 154

B

base classes, 96
binary operators, 29
bitwise operators, 31
blocks, 57
Bool values, 34
break statements, 79

C

capture list, 148
case clauses (switch statements), 75
    matching ranges in, 76
    using tuples in, 77
characters, 38
    literals, 19
Clang, 1
classes, 81-108
    computed properties, 85-86
    computed type properties, 89
    constant properties, 22, 89
    defining, 81
    deinitialization, 107
    inheritance, 96

initialization, 100-108
instances, 83
member protection, 95
methods, 90-95
nested types and, 20
overrides, preventing, 99
overriding superclass entities, 96-100
properties of, 84
properties, instance vs. type, 88
property observers, 87
self property, 92
stored properties, 84
subclassing, preventing, 99
closures, 57-63
    array algorithms as, 46
    automatic argument names, 59
    capturing values by reference, 62
    capturing values with, 60-62
    retain cycles and, 148
    trailing, 60
Cocoa Framework, 9
CollectionType protocol, 164
command line access, 6-8
comments, 14
Comparable protocol, 141, 153, 165
comparison operators, 33, 153
computed properties, 85-86
    extensions, 125
computed type properties, 89
computed variables, 23
conditionals, 73-80
    if-else statements, 73
    switch statements, 74-80
constant properties, 22
    in classes, 89
constants, 22
    default access level of, 121
    tuples, 27

continue statements, 79
convenience initializers, 101, 105
    overriding, 107
countElements(x) global function, 164
curly braces, 73
custom operators, 159
    precedence, 160

D

data types, 17-21
default clauses (switch statements), 75
deinitialization, 107
designated initializers, 101, 102-104
    overriding, 107
developer resources, 5
Developer Tools Access prompt, 7
dictionaries, 47-50
    accessing elements of, 48
    count property, 49
    isEmpty property, 49
    iterating over, 50
    keys property, 49
    modifying, 49
    mutable, 49
    properties of, 48
    remove all elements from, 49
    remove specified elements from, 50
    setting values for specified elements, 49
    updating values for specified elements, 49
    values property, 49
didSet keyword, 24
distanceTo() global function, 164
do-while loops, 72
downcasting, 129-131
    as operator, 35
    as? operator, 35

E

else clause, 74
enumerations, 112-119
    associated values, 116-117
    default access level of, 121
    methods in, 117
    raw member values, 114
    type methods in, 118
    using switch statements with, 80
Equatable protocol, 141
escaped characters in strings, 41
extensions, 123-126
    adopting protocols with, 136
    computed properties, 125
    default access level of, 122
    initializers, 125
    methods, 125
    subscripts, 126
external parameter names
    in init() methods, 104
    in methods, 91-92
external parameters names
    in functions, 53

F

filter() (arrays), 46
final keyword, 99
floating point literals, 18
for-condition-increment loops, 69
for-in loops, 71
    iterating over arrays with, 45
    iterating over dictionaries with, 50
ForwardIndexType protocol, 142
functions, 51-57
    computed variables, 23
    default access level of, 122
    default parameter values, 54
    external parameter names, 53
    generic, 149
    global, 163-168

local parameter names, 53
parameter types, 51
returning multiple values, 53
returning optional values, 52
returning tuples, 53
types, 56
variadic parameters for, 55

G

generics, 149-155
    constraining, 152-153
    default access level of, 122
    functions, 149
    protocols, 154-155
    types, 151
getter functions
    computed properties, 85
    computed variables, 23
    default access level of, 122
global functions, 163-168

H

half-open range operator, 35
Hashable protocol, 142

I

if-else statements, 73
    optional binding and, 65
import statements, 15
in-out parameters, 51
inheritance, 80, 96
    initializers and, 106-107
    protocols and, 137
initializer delegation, 111
initializers, 100-108
    convenience, 105
    default access level of, 122
    designated, 102-104
    extensions, 125
    for structures, 111
    inheritance and, 106-107
    overriding, 106

required, 107
instances, 83
instantiation, 83
Int types, 17
integer types, 17
    overflow operators, 34
internal access control level, 119
intervals, 161
iOS 7, 5
iOS 8, 5
is operator, 127
    checking for protocol con-
        formance, 140
    checking types with, 130
isEmpty(x) global function, 165

L

lambdas, 57
last(x) global function, 165
Lattner, Chris, 1
let statements, 65, 130
    value binding with, 78
literals
    array, 42
    character, 19
    dictionary, 47
    floating point, 18
    numeric, 18
    string, 19
LLDB, 1
LLVM, 1
local parameter names, 91-92
    in functions, 53
    in methods, 91-92
logical operators, 34
loops, 69-73
    do-while, 72
    early termination of, 73
    for-condition-increment, 69
    for-in, 71
    while, 72

M

map() (arrays), 46
max(list) global function, 165
maxElement(x) global function, 165
memberwise initializer, 111
memory leaks, 145
memory management, 142-149
    closures and, 148
    reference counting, 143
    retain cycles, 144, 148
    strong references, 144
    unowned references, 147
    weak references, 145
methods, 90-95
    extensions, 125
    in enumerations, 117
    in structures, 109
    optional in protocols, 134-136
    overriding, 99
    parameter names, local/external, 91-92
    required in protocols, 133
    self property and, 92
    subscripts, 93-95
    type, 93
min(x) global function, 165
minElement(x) global function, 165
mutable dictionaries, 49
MutableCollectionType protocol, 167
mutating methods, 110, 118, 125

N

nested types, 20
    default access level of, 123
null escape sequence, 41
numeric literals, 18

O

Objective-C, 1

operators, 29-38
    arithmetic, 30
    assignment, 32-33
    binary, 29
    binary, overloading, 156
    bitwise, 31
    comparison, 33
    custom, 159
    implicit type conversion, 30
    overflow, 34
    overloading, 155-159
    precedence, 36-38
    range, 35
    ternary, 29
    ternary conditional, 36
    type casting, 35
    unary, 29
    unary, overloading, 158
optional binding, 65
optional tuple return type, 53
optionals, 63-69
    as return value, 52
    chaining, 67-69
    implicitly unwrapped, 65
    method, 134-136
    Objective-C pointers vs., 63
    properties, 134-136
    testing value, 65
    unwrapping, 64
OS X 10.10 (Yosemite), 5
OS X 10.9 (Mavericks), 5
overflow operators, 31, 34
overridden superclass entities, 96-100
    accessing, 97
    initializers, 106
    methods, 99
    properties, 97-98
    subscripts, 99

P

parameters, function, 51
    default values for, 54

---

external names for, 53
local names for, 53
variadic, 55
Perl, 8
playground, 8-11
creating, 5
pointers
in Objective-C, 63
precedence
custom operators, 160
operators, 36-38
predecessor() global function, 165
prefixes, finding in strings, 40
print(x) global function, 166
Printable protocol, 142
println(x) global function, 166
private access control level, 119
program flow, 69-80
conditional execution, 73-80
loops, 69-73
properties
computed, 85-86, 125
computed type, 89
constant, 89
default access level of, 121
in structures, 109
instance vs. type, 88
optional in protocols, 134-136
overriding, 97-98
required in protocols, 132
stored, 84
property observers, 87
protocols, 131-142
adopting with extensions, 136
built-in, 141
checking conformance of, 140
default access level of, 123
generic, 154-155
inheritance and, 137
optional methods, 134-136
optional properties, 134-136
required methods, 133

required properties, 132
using as types, 138-140
public access control level, 119
Python, 8

Q
qsort() (C standard library), 57
Quick Look view (Xcode), 10

R
range operators, 35
RangeReplaceableCollectionType
protocol, 166
ranges, 160
matching, in case clauses, 76
value binding with, 78
raw values (enumerations), 114
reduce() (arrays), 46
reference counting, 143
removeAll(&x [, keepCapac-
ity:Bool]) global function, 166
removeAtIndex(&x, i: Index-
Type), 166
removeLast(&x) global function,
166
removeRange(&x, r: range) global
function, 166
required initializers, 107
required properties, 132
reserved words, 23
retain cycles, 144
return values
multiple, 53
optional, 52
tuples as, 28
reverse(x) global function, 166
arrays and, 47
Ruby, 8
Run-Evaluate-Print-Loop (REPL),
5, 6-8
starting, 7

S

scope
  capturing values by reference, 62
  closures and, 60-62
self property, 92
SequenceType protocol, 167
setter functions
  computed properties, 85
  computed variables, 23
  default access level of, 122
SignedNumberType protocol, 142
Sliceable protocol, 167
sort(&x) global function, 166
sort(&x, { closure }) global function, 167
sorted() function, 58
  on arrays, 47
sorted(x) global function, 167
sorted(x, { closure }) global function, 167
split(x, { closure }) global function, 167
statement labels, 79
stored properties, 84
Streamable protocol, 142
Strideable protocol, 142, 164
strides, 162
strings, 38-41
  comparing, 40
  countElements property, 39
  escaped characters in, 41
  hasPrefix comparison, 40
  hasSuffix comparison, 40
  interpolation, 41
  isEmpty property, 39
  literals, 19
  properties of, 39
  unicodeScalars property, 39
  utf16 property, 39
  utf8 property, 39
strong references, 144
structures, 108-112

initializers delegation in, 111
initializers for, 111
methods in, 109
mutating methods, 110
properties in, 109
type methods for, 110
subclass, 80
subclasses, 96-100
  default access level of, 123
subscripts, 93-95
  default access level of, 123
  extensions, 126
  overriding, 99
suffixes, finding in strings, 40
super prefix, 97
superclasses, 80
  deinitializer, inheritance of, 108
  initialization and, 100
  overriding entities, 96-100
  protocol inheritance and, 132
swap(&x, &y) global function, 168
Swift
  access control, 119-123
  arrays, 42-47
  as scripting language, 8
  classes, 81-108
  constants, 22
  data types, 17-21
  dictionaries, 47-50
  functions, 51-57
  generics, 149-155
  importing modules in, 15
  loops, 69-73
  memory management, 142-149
  operators, 29-38
  playground, 8-11
  program flow, 69-80
  protocols, 131-142
  reserved words, 23
  simple program in, 11-13

structures, 108-112
tuples, 26-29
variables, 21-26
Xcode, 5-11
switch statements, 74-80
matching ranges in case clauses, 76
statement labels, 79
using tuples in case clause, 77
using with enumerations, 80
value binding, 78
where qualifier, 78

T

ternary conditional operator, 36
ternary operator, 29
Timeline (Xcode), 10
toString(x) global function, 168
tuples, 26-29
as return type, 28
as return values, 53
constants, 27
default access level of, 123
extracting components of, 27
naming components, 28
using type aliases with, 28
value binding with, 78
variables, 27
type aliases, 20
default access level of, 123
using with tuples, 28
type casting operators, 35
type inferencing, 22
tuples and, 28
type methods
for structures, 110
in enumerations, 118
type placeholders, 150
typealias keyword, 20, 154
types, 17-21
aliases, 20
character literals, 19
checking, 128
downcasting, 129-131
generic, 151
integer, 17
nested, 20
numeric literals, 18
string literals, 19
using protocols as, 138-140

U

UIKit Framework, 9
UInt types, 17
unary operators, 29
overloading, 158
Unicode, 1
\u{n} arbitrary Unicode scalar character, 41
UnicodeScalars format of strings, 39
unowned references, 147
unwrapping optionals, 64
UTF-16, view of string in, 39
UTF-8, view of string in, 39

V

value types
arrays as, 43
dictionaries as, 48
strings as, 39
structures as, 108
var keyword
arrays and, 42
function parameters and, 51
value binding with, 78
variable parameters, 51
variables, 21-26
computed, 23
default access level of, 121
observers, 24-26
tuples, 27
variadic parameters, 55

W

weak references, 145
where qualifier, 78
while loops, 72
whitespace, 15
willSet keyword, 24
Worldwide Developers Conference (2014), 11

X

Xcode, 5-11
    multiple installs of, 6
    new projects, creating, 5
    playground, 8-11
    playground, creating, 5
    Swift REPL, 6-8
xcode-select command, 6

About the Author

Anthony Gray (you can call him Tony) has a long history working in tertiary education, where he's provided technical and systems support for academic and research staff, and for some very smart students. He loves to teach, with his favorite subjects being operating systems, computer graphics and animation with OpenGL, and most recently mobile development for iOS. In his spare time, he writes software to scratch his own itch, some of which is available at *squidman.net*. Secretly he pines for the days when you could handcode assembler for your 6502 and occasionally writes emulators so he can do just that.

Colophon

The animal on the cover of *Swift Pocket Reference* is an African palm swift (*Cypsiurus parvus*). This bird seeks palm trees for dwelling in the savannas and grasslands of sub-Saharan Africa and of the Arabian Peninsula. 16 centimeters in length, with a thin body and a long tail, the African palm swift is mostly brown with a gray throat and a black bill. Differences in coloring between genders (mostly in the tail) lessen with age. To avoid the ground, these birds use their short purple legs to cling to vertical surfaces.

The species's population appears to be on the rise, thanks largely to growth in the planting of the Washington palm tree.

Many of the animals on O'Reilly covers are endangered; all of them are important to the world. To learn more about how you can help, go to *animals.oreilly.com*.

The cover image is from Wood's *Illustrated Natural History*. The cover fonts are URW Typewriter and Guardian Sans. The text font is Adobe Minion Pro; the heading font is Adobe Myriad Condensed; and the code font is Dalton Maag's Ubuntu Mono.

The information you need, when and where you need it.

With Safari Books Online, you can:

Access the contents of thousands of technology and business books

- Quickly search over 7000 books and certification guides
- Download whole books or chapters in PDF format, at no extra cost, to print or read on the go
- Copy and paste code
- Save up to 35% on O'Reilly print books
- **New!** Access mobile-friendly books directly from cell phones and mobile devices

Stay up-to-date on emerging topics before the books are published

- Get on-demand access to evolving manuscripts.
- Interact directly with authors of upcoming books

Explore thousands of hours of video on technology and design topics

- Learn from expert video tutorials
- Watch and replay recorded conference sessions

safaribooksonline.com

O'REILLY®

Get even more for your money.

Join the O'Reilly Community, and register the O'Reilly books you own. It's free, and you'll get:

- $4.99 ebook upgrade offer
- 40% upgrade offer on O'Reilly print books
- Membership discounts on books and events
- Free lifetime updates to ebooks and videos
- Multiple ebook formats, DRM FREE
- Participation in the O'Reilly community
- Newsletters
- Account management
- 100% Satisfaction Guarantee

Signing up is easy:

1. Go to: oreilly.com/go/register
2. Create an O'Reilly login.
3. Provide your address.
4. Register your books.

Note: English-language books only

To order books online:
oreilly.com/store

For questions about products or an order:
orders@oreilly.com

To sign up to get topic-specific email announcements and/or news about upcoming books, conferences, special offers, and new technologies:
elists@oreilly.com

For technical questions about book content:
booktech@oreilly.com

To submit new book proposals to our editors:
proposals@oreilly.com

O'Reilly books are available in multiple DRM-free ebook formats. For more information:
oreilly.com/ebooks

O'REILLY®

CPSIA information can be obtained at www.ICGtesting.com
Printed in the USA
BVOW08n0114290515

402167BV00007B/4/P